Pechenga
(Petsamo)

● Murmansk

White Sea

Arkhangelsk ●

RUSSIAN FEDERATION

● Sortavala

Petrozavodsk ●
(Äänislinna)

*Lake
Onega*

Priozersk
(Käkisalmi/Kexholm)

*Lake
Ladoga*

St Petersburg
● *(Leningrad)*

0   100   200 miles

JONATHAN CLEMENTS is the author of a biography of Finland's most famous leader – *Mannerheim: President, Soldier, Spy* (Haus, 2009), as well as *A Brief History of the Vikings* (Robinson, 2005), and *An Armchair Traveller's History of the Silk Road* (Haus, 2013). He is currently a Visiting Professor at Xi'an Jiaotong University, China, but lives in Finland.

Armchair Traveller
at the bookHaus

An Armchair Traveller's History of Finland

Jonathan Clements

Armchair Traveller
at the bookHaus

First published in Great Britain in 2014 by
The Armchair Traveller at the bookHaus
70 Cadogan Place, London SW1X 9AH
www.thearmchairtraveller.com

Copyright © Jonathan Clements, 2014

All cartography produced by ML Design © Martin Lubikowski

Front cover image: *Hyökkäys* (The Attack), 1899, a painting by Edvard 'Eetu' Isto of the Maid of Finland being assaulted by the double-headed eagle of Russification. Copyright © National Board of Antiquities

A CIP catalogue record for this book is available from the British Library

ISBN: 978-1-909961-00-5
EBook ISBN: 978-1-909961-01-2

Typeset in Garamond by MacGuru Ltd
info@macguru.org.uk

Printed and bound in China by 1010 Printing International Ltd.

For my wife

Käy tulella taivaan ja loitsut kaikuen soi

Acknowledgements

Thanks to all those many Finns who have spoken to me about their country over the last few years, including those many anonymous guides and curators who were unable to resist recounting a few local stories for the mysterious foreign visitor. Thanks also to my two Finnish beta-readers and fact-checkers, Tino Warinowski and Johanna Ahonen, who have done their best to stop me from libelling anyone.

Other people who have contributed in some way to this book include Andrew Deacon, Harry Hall, Aino Haponen, Sanna Heikkinen, Nico Holmberg, Minna Janhonen, Risto Karinkanta, Pekka Kejo, Vantte & Elina Kilappa, Pekka Komu, Jussi Komulainen, Aleksi Laine, Teemu & Anna-Leena Korpijärvi, Lasse Lilja & Kaisa Aherto-Lilja, Elina Mattila, Samy Merchi, Jani Moliis, Kari Mäki-Kuutti, Kirsi Mäki-Kuutti, Matias Mäki-Kuutti, Pekka Mäki-Kuutti, Raija Mäki-Kuutti, Timo & Seija Mäki-Kuutti, Vitas & Jenni Mäki-Kuutti, Eija Niskanen, Raino & Elina Ojala, Anniina Ouramaa, Ritva 'Oolannin Sota' Parkkonen, Michael Peru-kangas, Juuso Pesälä, Anna Pitkänen, Salla Pösö, Ive Rii-himäki, Timo Riitamaa, Myry Voipio, Tuomas Saloniemi, Mari & Mikko Saario, Ellie Shillito, Leena Tarjamo, Niklas Vainio, Harri Virtanen, Myry Voipio, Olli Välke, and Marita von Weissenberg.

Contents

Introduction

THE PAINTING HANGS in the *Kansallismuseo*, the National Museum in Helsinki. It depicts a flaxen-haired girl in a white dress and blue scarf on a desolate, storm-tossed shore, clutching a massive book of laws. She is hanging on to it for dear life, while a double-headed eagle attempts to snatch it from her. The eagle's attack is already ripping the pages and warping the cover; it's not clear whether the book or its owner will survive this assault.

The painting is *Hyökkäys* (The Attack), completed in 1899 by the 34-year-old artist Edvard 'Eetu' Isto. The story goes that he began work on it in Berlin, but deliberately made the finishing touches in his Finnish homeland, the plight of which he was very pointedly symbolising.

The girl in blue and white is the Maid of Finland, a nationalist icon born in part from the shape made by the country of Finland itself, thought by some to resemble a girl in a dress with her arms outstretched. Her clothes, of course, invoke the blue cross of the country's thousands of lakes, on the white snowfield of the Finnish flag. The double-headed eagle represents Imperial Russia, the Tsar of which had also held the position of the Grand Prince of Finland. And the book of laws it is attacking represents almost a century of cordial rulership, in which Finns within the Russian Empire were allowed to use their own language, their own currency, and a limited form of autonomous self-government. Things were changing, and would never quite be the same again.

Hyökkäys was a stark piece of propaganda, part of a massive upswelling of Finnish nationalism that gripped the country in the late 19th century. It would end, eventually, in the revolution of 1917, in which Finland became the only former territory of the Russian Empire to evade Soviet takeover.

For the historically-minded reader in search of insight into Finland and the Finns, *Hyökkäys* and the National Romantic sensibility that birthed are part of a pivotal moment. Its artists and authors wrestled with the very nature of 'Finnishness,' a concept that had often been ignored or glossed over by two sets of foreign masters. This book similarly follows the Finns' own developing sense of themselves, from hunters and crofters regarded as little more than savages by conquering Swedes, to the initially loyal and welcoming subjects of the Tsar after the Grand Duchy was handed over to Russia. It continues through the turbulent 20th century, in which Finland was born from the fires of revolution and a bitter civil war, only to be forced to fight for its life in the Winter War, the Continuation War and the Lapland War.

Because Finland is such a young country, many of its heroes and icons are relatively recent creations. The seasoned traveller among the Finns will often spy elements of Swedish or Russian culture, which no Finn will ever believe could not be ineffably Finnish, but also traditions that are less remembered than they are invented or recreated. Paramount among them is the Finnish national myth, the *Kalevala*, one of the first and most influential of many European epics to appear in the nationalist 19th century.

With a notoriously difficult language, a legendarily stubborn population, a political scene that aspires to socialist utopia, and international fame for sitting naked in hot, steamy sheds, the people of Finland have an odd reputation. But with the aid of this book, you will see much more of Finland and the Finns – you will hear their own jokes about themselves, and read the words of their songs, and understand the way they view the world.

It has been over a decade since I first accidentally went to Finland and inadvertently stayed. When I was asked to write an Armchair Traveller's History, I set about writing a book that covered the subjects I wish I had known about before I arrived, and which pointed at the many items of interest that all too often pass the preoccupied tourist by. This book is the result.

From the Fenni to Lalli: Prehistory to 1159

T HE ROAD LEADS to part of Lake Köyliö in south-west
Finland, near the village that also bears that name,
winding downhill through a forest park, some distance from
the island church. The statue itself seems nondescript and
anonymous. From a distance, you'd be forgiven for thinking
it was a soldier, standing almost to attention, his left hand
holding a long spear. The man is larger than life, clad in furs
with a bulky hat more likely to be associated today with the
Russian Arctic. In his other hand, resting against his thigh,
is a tangle of straps and slats – old-fashioned snow shoes.
He holds an axe under his armpit, as if just about to don the
shoes, but keeping his weapon close at hand.

One wonders how much fun the Finns have with local
visitors, asking them who they think the statue represents.
Is it a war memorial? Is it some famous Russian trapper? Is
it Mannerheim (if in doubt, say it's Mannerheim), that most
famous of Finns, his officer's moustache grown out into
a bushy beard on some long mission? Is it a famous Arctic
explorer, clutching some kind of harpoon, ready to take on
an unlucky whale?

It was sculpted by Aimo Tukiainen in 1989, commissioned
by the local bank, Köyliön Säästöpankki, in celebration of
its centenary. You will hear things like this a lot in Finland,
a country young enough that not only the subjects, but also

the initiators of its public artworks are still acknowledged. The Finns, perhaps more than many other nations, appreciate the value and use of public art. The statues you see are there for a reason, and the reason is often relatively recent – some bank or factory with a desire to commemorate itself by siting itself in older traditions. In this case, the bank chose to make a name for itself by commissioning a statue of an illiterate, brawling country bumpkin, infamously henpecked husband and notorious murderer. The statue is of a man who may never have even existed, called Lalli.

The Martyrdom of Saint Henry

There are many conflicting stories about Lalli. The original, basic version may not have even given him a name, but during the later Middle Ages the tale was augmented, accreting additional data like a rolling snowball. However it begins, it ends the same way, sometime around AD 1155, with Lalli, a dim-witted Finnish forester, accosting the saintly Bishop Henry of Uppsala on the winter ice of Köyliö lake. There is a misunderstanding – in the most embroidered of versions, Lalli's wife Kerttu has told him that the Bishop came to stay, ate their food, drank their drink, and left 'nothing but ashes'. Lalli swings his axe, and murders the defenceless Henry, inadvertently creating Finland's first martyr, and its patron saint.

Lalli hacks off Henry's finger to get at his papal ring. He sticks the Bishop's mitre on his head. He rifles through Henry's positions and returns home to the shrewish Kerttu, boasting of his deed. But when he tries to take the holy hat off, part of his scalp comes with it. His remaining hair starts falling out in clumps. He tries to take off the ring, but it strips the flesh from his finger, leaving only bone. Lalli eventually goes mad, and drowns himself in the lake.

Meanwhile, Henry's servants come out of hiding. It is implied that he had ordered them to take refuge in the forest, seemingly in the knowledge that Lalli had murderous intent. According to Henry's wishes, they gather up his remains and wrap them in cloth tied with blue string. Laid on a cart, they are pulled along by a stallion, until it gives up. This is then replaced by an ox. Where the ox stops, a church is built in Henry's memory.

In distant Götaland, Sweden, a priest heard the story of Henry's demise, and made some sort of wisecrack about it. He immediately developed an ominous stomach ache. Before long, more obviously *miraculous* phenomena began to occur. Two children supposedly rose up from the dead in Finland. A group of sailors prayed to Henry and were saved from a storm. In nearby Kyrö, a lame man walked and a blind woman saw.

By the end of the 13th century, Henry, Bishop of Uppsala, was known as Saint Henry, the 'Bishop of Finland', although he had never held that post in life. His unassuming stone cross on Kirkkokari Island in Lake Köyliö has become the start site of Finland's only Catholic pilgrimage, *Henrikin tie* (Henry's Road), along which believers annually walk the 140 kilometres from the site of his martyrdom to Nousiainen, the site of his alleged burial. On this journey, which ends the night before Midsummer's Eve, travellers are entertained with the *Death-Lay of Henry*, which recounts the events of his life, death and miracles, in a considerably more sensational fashion than his medieval *Vita Henricus*.

> Now the bishop is in joy, Lalli in evil torture.
> The bishop sings with the angels, performs a joyful
>   hymn.
> Lalli is skiing down in hell. His left ski slides along,
> Into the thick smoke of torture. With his staff he strikes
>   about him:
> Demons beset him cruelly. In the swelter of hell
> They assail his pitiful soul.

But there is no statue of Henry at Köyliö. It's his murderer who gets the permanent memorial, at least in part because Henry was a foreigner. He was a bishop from Uppsala in Sweden, but was widely believed to have come from England. Garbled references refer to his youth in Cabbage-land (*Kaalimaa*), a non-existent location that has puzzled Finns for centuries. However, any medieval historian is sure to recognise it from an infamous insult directed by Olaf the Stout at poor King Canute about the English food he had to eat.

Perhaps there was never a real Henry, either. Like so many other martyrs from before the Congregation on the Causes of Saints in 1588, his canonisation was never officially declared, nor was any diligent Vatican investigator put on his case. The Catholic Church has no record of a Henry of Uppsala that fits in with his timeline, and neither does the Bishopric of Uppsala. It is true that there were English missionaries among the Swedes in the 'New Land' to the east of the Gulf of Bothnia, and indeed likely that more Englishmen rose to prominence in the Church during the reign of the English Pope Adrian IV (r.1154–1159). Although 'Saint' Henry was barely even recognised or celebrated outside Finland, Sweden and a couple of parishes in north Germany, he achieved his popularity because, in the eyes of the Finnish devout, his story was, at least, local. Finns could point at Lake Köyliö, where he was supposedly killed; they could visit Kyrö, where his early miracles manifested. They could claim him as their own.

Lalli, however, was a different matter. He *was* a local. He was a Finn who stood up, in some misguided way, to the imposition of authority by Swedish masters. As the years passed, particularly whenever Finns debated 'Finnishness,' Lalli cropped up frequently as an icon of all that was not-Swedish, not-foreign, not-Catholic. The statue in Köyliö carefully redacts his iconic image as a thug murdering a holy man, presenting him instead with all the accoutrements otherwise implied by the story: the fur clothes of a trapper, the snowshoes of a wintry landscape, and the axe of a forester. At the most basic of levels, Lalli reduces Finnishness to simple woodland life in a freezing environment, with a little bit of bloody-minded, murderous resistance to authority thrown in. He is the first of the Finns.

Prehistory & Early Finns

> In wonderful savageness lives the nation of the Fenni, and in beastly poverty, destitute of arms, of horses, and of homes; their food, the common herbs; their apparel, skins; their bed, the earth; their only hope in their arrows, which for want of iron they point with bones. Their common support they have from the chase, women as well as men; for with these the former wander up and down, and crave a portion of the prey. Nor other shelter have they even for their babes, against the violence of tempests and ravening beasts, than to cover them with the branches of trees twisted together ...

So wrote the Roman author Tacitus in his *Germania* (c. AD 98), identifying a tribe far to the frozen north. Fifty years later, in the *Geographia* (c. AD 150), the Alexandrian author Claudius Ptolemy similarly alluded to a tribe he called the Phinnoi, found in two separate locations in Scandia and Sarmatia. Both seem in agreement that wherever these Finns are to be found, their life seems rather miserable. This is a recurring concept in discussions of Finland, a land so far removed from the norms of established culture that its critics have often found it wanting.

'Foreigners are conceited and envious,' complained Daniel Juslenius in 1700, 'they foolishly believe that there is no civilisation beyond the confines of their own country, and particularly not in these regions, which they have never seen. Indeed, they boast that their cabins are taller than our towers.'

Humans came relatively late to Finland, since the entire region was buried under ice until only 12,000 years ago. In geological terms, the last of the Ice Ages left Finland so recently that the land is still bouncing back up – lifting in relief after the weight of the snows, and rising fast. Many are the places in Finland where a town named as a harbour, or a mansion named for a beachside view, seem oddly far inland. Many are the historical town records in which townsfolk complain their harbour has become unsuitable, particularly in the north of the Gulf of Bothnia. There, in the 18th century, Anders Celsius conducted scientific experiments, and discovered that the coastal land was rising at the geological pell-mell pace of 13mm a year. By the year AD 4000, the north of the Bay of Bothnia will be a freshwater lake, walled off by a new ridge across its middle.

Archaeological evidence of the first inhabitants of Finland is largely lost, drowned or scraped away by several last gasps of the Ice Age that rolled back over the earliest places of habitation. There is only one place in the region that has offered possible evidence of earlier habitation, and that is the controversial Susiluola (Wolf Cave) near Karijoki, where archaeologists in 1996 found what may have been evidence of Neanderthal inhabitants some 120,000 years ago. This suggests there were inhabitants in the area *between* the Riss and Würm Ice Ages. However, Susiluola has become a matter of academic dispute, with some refusing to believe that the limited finds of flint chips are man-made at all, and others arguing that the cave would have been underwater at the time the finds were supposedly left there.

Sometime around 7200 BC, someone left a bone ice pick, a fish net and a ski runner near the site of modern Lahti. Hunters were converging on Finland from both the south and possibly north, from the Norwegian coast.

In Suomusjärvi, now part of Salo in south-west Finland, archaeologists found a Stone Age area of settlement, occupied for around 2,000 years after 6500 BC by humans who subsisted on hunting and fishing. Bone evidence and surviving artefacts suggest that their main prey were seals, perhaps not dissimilar to the endangered Saimaa ringed seal, only 310 of which currently survive – the last descendants of marine mammals left landlocked by the fast-rising lake land.

The world of these Stone Age people was very different, scattered not with the birch and firs of modern Finland, but with hazel, elm and oak. By 4200 BC, these primitive inhabitants were starting to settle, and trading with nearby tribes. The Comb-Ceramic culture, whose distinctive pots are found across a wide swathe of Europe, made inroads into the Finnish area, and these early users of stone tools began importing a better class of stone from the east – evidence survives in eastern Finland not only of tools made from Russian flint, but of entire slabs of green schist brought from Lake Onega, and wooden spoons made from a pine that only grows near the Urals. We have no idea what the Finns traded for such goods, but later accounts, particularly in Viking sagas, suggest that one of the things that Finland was best known for was animal pelts.

Finland entered the Bronze Age around 1500 BC, when the metal is first found, not mined locally, but brought in as another import. By this time, the archaeological evidence suggests, the Finns had turned to limited farming to supplement their hunting culture, although animal husbandry was more important for them.

So much of the material culture of this period was made from substances that readily decompose. Evidence suggests that all of Finland, along with the rest of the Nordic region, was widely but sparsely settled by the end of the Stone Age, but that the isolated tribes of reindeer herders and seal hunters had a culture much as Tacitus would later describe – of skin tents and wooden utensils, little of which has survived. At some point during the Bronze Age, there was a palpable split between the cultures. Some continued to follow the reindeer herds in the north, living a nomadic existence. Others cleared forest areas and focused on farming. Although the two groups remained closely inter-related, with regular contact and many shared beliefs, their languages began to diverge. We can still hear two accents on what is essentially the same word, used by each of the groups to identify themselves. The herders called their land Sapmi; the farmers called theirs Suomi.

Tacitus thought that the people of Sapmi had the better idea:

> Such a condition they judge more happy than the painful idea of cultivating the ground, than the labour of rearing houses, than the agitations of hope and fear attending the defence of their own property or the seizing of that of others. Secure against the designs of men, secure against the malice of the gods, they have accomplished a thing of infinite difficulty; that to them, nothing remains even to be wished.

The Rome of Tacitus was a world away from the Finns, although fragments of it did make their way to the far north. A handful of Roman coins have been dug up on Finnish sites, as well as two wine ladles, a glass drinking horn and a gold bracelet. These items, as well as several swords of Mediter-ranean origin, appear to have drifted up to Finland through the tribes of Germany, rather than being traded directly with any foolhardy or enterprising Roman merchants.

The Vikings & Balagard

By the Dark Ages, the people of the Suomi farmlands had advanced further to the north, pushing the 'Saami' people of Sapmi out of what is now Tampere and Hämeenlinna. It is possible, although difficult to prove, that this period is the source of certain references in Finnish folklore to *Pohjola* (the Northland), a rival realm ruled by a wise but vindictive witch-queen, ever at odds with the homespun heroes of Finnish epics.

Slash-and-burn cultivation was the rule – with forest areas cleared, crops sown for several seasons, and the land then abandoned to grow over once more with trees. The Finnish settlers had to contend with visitations from the north and west, as sailors from what is now Norway and Sweden ventured into the lakes. It was in Finland that Norse seamen are liable to have learned one of their most crucial and transferable skills. The skerries and islets of the archipelago in southwest Finland gave way to landlocked lakes and rivers, but *portage*, in which a ship's crew clambers out and bodily hefts their vessel over a ridge or rapids, opened much of Finland's hinterland to explorers, traders and raiders. By the time we first hear of the semi-legendary foundation of a 'Viking' state in what is now Russia, around the middle of the 9th century AD, it is likely that the rowers who ventured there sailed along a Gulf of Finland that was already either well-settled with homesteads, or entirely picked over for plunder.

Archaeological evidence, once more, is scant, but points to settlers and traders from Sweden. Viking swords have been found as far to the east as Kiviniemi, while in 1686, diggers in Uskela (now part of Salo) uncovered a hoard of coins from the Arab world and the England of Ethelred the Unready. Inexplicably tucked away in a corner of the Museum of Central Finland, in Jyväskylä, amid all the anonymous canoes and milk churns, is a striking Viking-era necklace, worn by some long-forgotten lady of what was plainly a culturally Scandinavian settlement.

Viking sagas might allude to 'kings' and chieftains in the lands of lakes and snow, although notably the word in Finnish for a king (*kuningas*) is a foreign borrowing, as if the Finns themselves never had much of a use for it. But there are occasional leaders of the Finns whose names are mentioned in old legends. Daniel Juslenius writes of the Finnish 'king' Rostioff, 'who was worshipped as a god by the Swedes after his death', and the feisty princess Skjalv. Dragged back to Sweden as a concubine of King Ingemar, who had killed her father King Froste, Skjalv bided her time and eventually strangled Ingemar with a golden chain. The *Heimskringla*, chronicle of the Norwegian kings, goes into greater detail:

> Now when King Agne had got drunk, Skjalv bade him take care of his gold torc which he had about his neck; therefore he took hold of the ornament, and bound it fast about his neck before he went to sleep. The land-tent stood at the wood side, and a high tree over the tent protected it against the heat of the sun. Now when King Agne was asleep, Skjalv took a noose, and fastened it under the ornament. Thereupon her men threw down the tent-poles, cast the loop of the noose up in the branches of the tree, and hauled upon it, so that the king was hanged close under the branches and died; and Skjalv with her men ran down to their ships, and rowed away.

Far more common in saga sources are references to sorcerers and witches with some Finnish connection, but their provenance is doubtful, as is their location. The Norse skalds would used the term 'Finn' to refer to both Saami and Suomi peoples of what is now Finland, so many of the tales from the sagas take place in a vague area somewhere between northern Norway and Russia.

Norse sailors made it as far as the Tammer rapids, the site of modern Tampere, where one more heave of a ship up the steep slope would open up the multiple routes through northern lakes. The site of Tampere's modern airport, Pirk-kala, still bears a name that may derive from *Birca*, the Birch Island trading post of old Sweden, evoking images of ships pulled ashore, campfires and haggling over furs. This Norse presence is marked, in a typically Finnish fashion, with a statue not of the visitors, but of the type of local who greeted them – the Hunter, one of four statues by Wäinö Aaltonen on Tampere's modern Hämeensilta bridge, in which a bronze, naked man holds out an animal skin. To this day, the word in Finnish for money is *raha* (literally 'pelt'), and *oravannahka* (squirrel-skin) is a jocular slang term for cash.

The Vikings adapted their sea-borne methods for river travel, seizing islands mid-stream or mid-lake as naturally-defended bases. Somewhere in what is now Finland, there was an island fort, called *Balagard* (possibly 'Meadow Fort') by the Dark Age Scandinavians, but its location is unclear. Ice and changing water levels have probably long done for any material evidence of it, leaving much discussion of Finland in Viking sagas a matter of vague generalities. The land of the Finns crops up in occasional stories, where trips in search of 'tribute' from the forest region lead to the extraction of furs and pelts from the huntsmen. Finland also seemed to be a place of piracy and adventure, where several Danish and Norwegian rulers sailed in search of their fortunes, usually at the expense of the local residents.

The youngest child of Siward, King of the Geats, the princess Alvild, for example, was said to walk everywhere veiled by her cloak, in order to hide her fabled beauty from unwelcome suitors. Her father did his bit to protect his daughter's chastity by posting armed guards outside her chambers and, just to be sure, giving her two poisonous snakes to keep as pets – these deadly creatures forming the last line of defence.

The story, purporting to refer to events in the 5th century AD, appears in Saxo Grammaticus's *History of the Danes* as well as Olaus Magnus's *Description of the Northern Peoples* – the latter largely rips off the former. Both versions seem a little garbled, with Alvild's guardians soon repurposed not as a protection from suitors, but as a *test* that suitors must over-come. True to the tradition of difficult father-in-laws in many cultures, Siward promises his daughter's hand to anyone who can run the gauntlet, although any who give up halfway will be beheaded and have their heads stuck on a spike.

The Danish prince Alf somehow makes it through and slays the snakes with a red-hot spear-point, seemingly to Alvild's delight. However, in what also seems oddly mangled and counter-intuitive, at least so far as the tale endures today, Alvild's mother upbraids her for being so shallow as to like a man merely for his looks (and snake-slaying capabilities), and persuades her to renounce all suitors, disguise herself in men's clothes, and run away to become a pirate.

She manages this by handily stumbling across a group of Vikings who have just lost their leader, and who inexplicably decide that a freshly-arrived princess would make an ideal replacement. She then marauds all along the coast of Finland, until one fateful day on its south-western tip, off the Hanko peninsula (the only time an actual Finnish place-name crops up), she spies a rival fleet heading towards the port. Alvild orders her fleet onto the attack, in a fierce battle of locked oars and onboard swordplay.

Despite, it is implied, numerous victories in her Viking career, Alvild finally meets her match, when the rival Viking leader storms aboard her ship accompanied by overwhelming numbers of fresh warriors. But when his lieutenant Borkar knocks off Alvild's helmet, Alf, for it is he, realises the true identity of his foe.

> [Alf], as soon as he saw the delicacy of her countenance, realised that they should be going to work with kisses, not with weapons; they should lay aside their hard spears and handle their foe with more persuasive attentions.

In something of an anti-climax, at least for me, Alf immediately sticks Alvild back in a dress and drags her home to live happily ever after – their daughter, Gurith, becoming one of the ancestors of the kings of Denmark.

THE 11TH-CENTURY CHRONICLER Adam of Bremen, like many fellow authors who touched on Finnish subjects, was keener on pointing out that the people of Lapland were pagan sorcerers:

> These people, it is said, are to this day so superior in the magic arts or incantations that they profess to know what everyone is doing the world over. Then they also draw great sea monsters to shore with a powerful mumbling of words and do much else of which one reads in the Scriptures about magicians. All this is easy for them through practice. I have heard that women grow beards in the extremely rough alps of that region, and that the men live in the woods, rarely exposing themselves to sight.

Adam is on his own in his account of bearded ladies, but he was the inheritor of a long tradition of tall tales about Finnish wizardry, much of which can be found in the Viking sagas. There are garbled tales, preserved among the ancient manuscripts of Iceland, of 'Finns' who could leave their bodies in a drug-induced trance, flying in the form of birds of prey, or making long voyages in the form of whales.

Finnvitka, the 'making of witchcraft,' seems to have been the preserve of the people of Lapland, such that in modern Swedish, the phrase 'pay a visit to the Finns' survives as a term for visiting a fortune teller. In *Heimskringla*, the chronicle of the kings of Norway, it's a Lappish witch who foretells the colonisation of Iceland, and a group of shape-shifting Saami shamans who reconnoitre the island as whales before the trip is approved.

Perhaps the most famous graduate of the Finnish wizardry school was Gunnhild Kingsmother, supposedly a 10th century woman of royal Scandinavian birth, who was packed off to Lapland to learn magic from Saami shamans. Depending on which saga one believes, she was either staying as a guest with 'Motull, King of the Finns,' or living in some sort of sexualised bondage in a shack with two predatory warlocks. Either way, she ran into the ominously-named Erik Bloodaxe, who whisked her away back to Norway, where he eventually became king, as would their son Harald Greycloak.

Gunnhild looms large in many of the most famous Icelandic sagas, where she is often depicted as a spiteful termagant. It has been suggested that her Finnish origins, coming from the mysterious and feral lands of the north and east, were concocted by later writers in order to both explain her bad behaviour, and to help shift the blame on to her for political decisions that were actually made by her husband.

The Newborn King

There is a marked change to the archaeological record in Finland in the Middle Ages, as a palpable *absence* sweeps from west to east across the country. Sometime around the middle of the 11th century, the people of the Åland Islands in the Baltic stopped burying their dead with grave goods. Whereas bodies had previously been accompanied by artefacts for use in the afterlife – swords and armour, farming implements and spinning paraphernalia, even sometimes animal sacrifices – now archaeologists were lucky to find anything in a grave beyond a simple necklace with a crucifix.

Only a few decades later, the same practice arrived in southwest Finland ('Finland Proper', as it is still called), where the Swedish settlers seemed to give up on paganism. Some pagan graveyards were abandoned altogether. Others instead gained a grander new centrepiece, in the form of a Christian church, defiantly situated on top of all the ancestors, both breaking with the old ways and claiming to inherit them.

Within a hundred years, the new religion had spread up into Tavastia – the old name for the long reach of lands towards Hämeenlinna and Tampere. However, burial practices further to the east, in Karelia, remained pagan until around 1300.

Many centuries later, the folklorist Elias Lönnrot (see Chapter 3) would collate some of the surviving tales, songs and poems from Karelia that alluded to the arrival of Christianity with confusion. His *Kalevala* collection ends with the song-cycle of the 'Newborn King', in which a pious virgin called Marjatta eats a magical berry that makes her pregnant, is cast out by her scandalised family, and gives birth to a child prodigy that the sun and moon praise as being their own creator.

She goes off to Väinämöinen, the Finnish hero, to ask him what she should do, and he sternly orders that the baby be thrown in a swamp. The child then speaks, upbraiding Väinämöinen and calling him a stupid old man whose time has passed. After a tongue-lashing that lasts for a couple of pages, Väinämöinen gets into his boat and sails away in a huff. It is supposedly a happy ending, in which the Christ-child brings light to the forests, and the old ways depart leaving only their music, but Väinämöinen's parting words bear about them an element of prophecy and curse – a rather confident prediction that the time will come when the Finns will call him back.

> Suns may rise and set in Suomi,
> Rise and set for generations,
> When the North will learn my teachings,
> Will recall my wisdom-sayings,
> Hungry for the true religion.
> Then will Suomi need my coming,
> Watch for me at dawn of morning,
> That I may bring back the Sampo,
> Bring anew the harp of joyance,
> Bring again the golden moonlight,
> Bring again the silver sunshine,
> Peace and plenty to the Northland.

Before political authority arrived from Sweden on the point of a sword, the forests and farms of Finland experienced a slow and unstoppable rise of Christian conversion, washing from west to east.

Elements of Christianity were first intermixed with Finland's original pagan religion, and survive in many folktales and spells that modern-day Finns might sheepishly prefer to call prayers. There are stories that Christ arrived among the trees, and baptised the son of Tapio, Finland's god of the forests. Jesus, or Christ (but never Jesus Christ), and Mary are often invoked in cantrips for healing wounds, staving off gossips or warding off evil.

Lönnrot's *Magic Songs of the Finns* (1880) recorded all these atavisms, still recounted in the wilds of Karelia in his day, as well as many mixtures of half-understood tales of Christian saints with half-remembered tales of pagan gods. A spell for luring otters into traps conflates Christopher, 'the golden king of rivers' with a Finnish river god. Tahvanus, the god of horses, is conflated with Tapani, the Finnish pronunciation of Stephen, in a spell that exhorts Saint Stephen to watch over a group of horses. Juhannes, the 'best of priests', refuses to baptise the children of the witch-queen of Lapland, but supposedly christens fire itself, turning the fiery pyres of every Finnish midsummer's eve from a pagan festival into a Christian celebration.

Surviving stories from the fall of paganism also allude to the growing power of the Christian community, and the sense that baptism eventually became not only desirable, but a prospect that could be withheld from the undeserving. One snippet contains a warning from an exorcist to an evil spirit, suggesting that:

> If thou shouldst injure a Christian man or destroy a man
> that is baptised, christening perchance will injure thee,
> baptism will haply thee destroy.

Already, the story was spreading that Lalli had paid dearly for his murderous assault on Bishop Henry. There would surely be other martyrdoms in the expansion of Christianity into the forests, but the priests were soon followed by crusaders and colonists. As the kingdom of Sweden advanced ever eastward, and the proto-Russian state of Novgorod pushed westwards to meet it, the Finns were caught in the middle. They faced contending forms of Christianity and allegiance that would buffet them for the next thousand years.

2

East of Sweden: 1159–1809

IN THE TOWN SQUARE of Vyborg, in what is now Russia, there is a statue of a noble-looking warrior. He stands proud, his sword held nonchalantly, blade-down, like a walking stick, his chest raised as if preparing to bellow out a command to the castle on the other side of the nearby strait. His helmet has an odd crest to it, and his face is a sea-dog scramble of beard and moustache.

This is Torkel Knutsson (d.1306), a Swedish military leader, who chose this spot to build a coastal island-fortress like the Viking strongholds of old. Torkel had led what is now usually known as the Third Swedish Crusade, pushing back the peoples of Novgorod and establishing a new border for Sweden many hundreds of miles further to the east than it sits today. The area was hotly contested for many centuries to come, and indeed, was not even acknowledged as Swedish territory until a generation after Torkel's death. The statue was raised in 1908, in what was then the Finnish city of Viipuri, but removed and sequestered in a cupboard in 1944. Now it is back in full view, gazing proudly at the nearby castle.

The Imaginary Crusades

The 'First' Swedish Crusade, in which Saint Henry sup-posedly met his end, remains a matter of conjecture. Quite possibly it never happened, or is a ridiculously hopeful, pious spin on far more mundane raids and expeditions into the Finnish marches. The incorporation of Finland, officially and politically, into Swedish territory, did not truly occur until around 1249, when Birger Magnusson (c.1200–66), 'Duke of the Swedes,' led a campaign among the lakes, recorded a century later in a German chronicle as the official date of the pacification of the Finnish lands, bringing them under Swedish authority. It was only then, with Finland secure, that Swedish legends began backdating this acquisition, rebranding Birger's achievements as a 'Second' Crusade in the footsteps of a mythical first.

Sweden appears to have embarked upon this large-scale deception to scare off potential competitors. Since Finland was, to all intents and purposes, unclaimed wilderness, it might appear to be fair game to representatives from any number of kingdoms. The Swedes were not alone – their expeditions had to contend with similar forays by the kingdom of Denmark, which eventually concentrated on the southern shore of the Gulf of Finland. Meanwhile, the proto-Russian state of Novgorod was expanding westwards into the same territory. Largely forgotten in all the posturing and combat of the period is the contribution of the Germans, whose Hanseatic League of merchants enjoyed powerful trading connections all along the Baltic coasts, without seeking any particular political power.

These merchants, largely from Saxony and Westphalia, who began arriving in southern Finland with artefacts of technology and culture in the 13th century, have left very little evidence of their presence, although Finnish slang of the period referred to any item of intricacy or wonder as *saksa* (which is to say, 'German'). It's the Germans who are thought to have built the first church in Turku, and who supplied much of the trade goods that flowed into south-west Finland to make culture there possible in the first place.

Sweden's sudden decision to pretend to have been running around in the forests, Bible in one hand and sword in the other, for the previous hundred years or so, should be taken in the context of these contending cultural influences, as a long-term move designed to keep the Danes and Germans away from the Finnish shores. In this, they were successful, so much so that many Finns are not aware that there was any competition at all.

A 'Third' Crusade duly followed, although as ever, the term 'crusade' seems overly hopeful, and was often retroactively applied to random skirmishes and occasional sallies in the centuries-long to-and-fro between the peoples of Sweden and their rivals in Novgorod. So it is that we have the chronicles of the Russians recording a stirring victory against the 'Swedes' in 1240, when Prince Alexander Nevsky gained his surname for utterly destroying the enemy at the Battle of the River Neva. As related in the *First Chronicle of Novgorod*:

> Swedes came with a great army, and Norwegians and Finns and Tavastians with ships in great numbers, and they stayed on the Neva ... willing to take [Lake] Ladoga, and to put it short, Novgorod and all of its lands. But still protected the merciful, man-loving God and sheltered us from the foreign people ... Prince Alexander did not hesitate at all, but went against them with Novgorodians and people of Ladoga ... And a great number of them fell; and when [the Swedes] had loaded two ships with the bodies of high-born men, they let them sail to the sea; but the others that were unnumbered, they cast to a pit, that they buried; and many others were wounded; and that same night they fled, without waiting for the Monday night, with shame.

This will be news to anyone reading similar chronicles from Sweden, which make no mention of any crusade, nor any great battle, let alone a great defeat on the Neva. The Swedes at the time were far too busy fighting a war amongst themselves about the rightful heir to the Swedish throne, making it highly unlikely that anyone would be in a position to mount a large expedition against the Russians.

Notably, the chronicle mentions 'Tavastians,' people from the central Finland region near what is now Hämeenlinna and Tampere. Only three years earlier, in 1237, a papal letter to the archbishop of Uppsala had suggested that the Swedes go on a crusade *in Tavastia*, to protect Christian settlers from raiders – possibly from Novgorod, but more likely other Finns. This seems to run in the same tradition as an earlier papal admonition, from 1172, which complained about the number of fair-weather Christians in Finland, happy to continue their pagan ways when life was good, but whining to the nearest bishop that they were under threat whenever attacked by raiders. A place-name in modern Finland is a distant echo of such prevarications – Katumajärvi, near modern Hämeenlinna, literally translates as 'Lake of Regret,' and is thought to have been the place where locals would wash off the taint of their Christian baptism after their crusader rescuers retreated once more to the south.

On the basis of all this evidence, or lack of it, it seems reasonable to suggest that the Finnish hinterland remained as uncontrolled and subject to changes in authority as it had done during the Viking era. Isolated pockets were claimed by Novgorod, although such an advance led to claims in Sweden that Novgorodians had 'attacked' Swedish territory. The next season, Swedes would take back 'their' town or trading post, only for the Novgorodians to report the act as an attack by raiders. Any Finnish settlers caught in the middle would be buffeted by seasonal changes in allegiance, told first that they were Eastern Orthodox Russians, and then that they were Catholic Swedes. A picky historian might also note that when Alexander Nevsky led an army that included 'people of Ladoga' against an army that included 'Tavastians,' he was essentially leading one group of ethnic Finns against another.

In the 1290s, Torkel Knutsson seized the river-mouth sites of Vyborg and Kexholm, fortifying them in old-fashioned Viking style with a fort on a river island. His decision was a matter of strategy and geography, since the two sites represented the two water courses of the Vuoksi river system. Whoever held Vyborg and Kexholm guarded the river route into Lake Saimaa, and hence the gateway to the Finnish hinterland.

But Torkel's seizures, of what had previously been Novgorod settlements, and (who knows?) maybe Swedish settlements once more before that, were not ratified until 1323, with the signature of a treaty between Sweden and Novgorod. It had no particular name at the time, but is usually known today as the Treaty of Nöteborg or Pähkinäsaari, the Swedish and Finnish names respectively for an island fort on the shore of Lake Ladoga. Tellingly, the treaty was not brokered by either side, but by exasperated Hanseatic merchants, who were plainly sick of the unsure political situation in the area. At the urging of the Germans, the Swedes and Russians settled on a mutually-agreed border, which roughly extended from the south-eastern corner of the Gulf of Finland, near the site of what is today St Petersburg, in a straight line to Oulu on the Baltic coast.

The Pähkinäsaari line established the cultural sphere of old Finland, although it barely encompasses a third of the country as we know it today. If the border were restored in modern times, it would exclude all of Lapland from Finnish authority, as well as Karelia and Kainuu – the towns of Kajaani, Iisalmi and Kuhmo would be on the wrong side. It was only the southern end of the line that bothered the signatories, as it established a peaceful environment in the Vyborg area. The northern end was really of no concern to anyone, but established for the next 300 years the idea that the Karelia and Lapland area remained wilderness, free for both Russians and Swedes to exploit.

People of the Österland

The Finns are phantoms throughout 600 years of Swedish history. The reader is often left wondering, when reading of 'Swedish' settlers in America, or 'Swedish' sailors encountered in foreign ports, to what extent the people described are actually Swedes from the *Österland* (Eastland) which is to say, Finns. As Swedish subjects, the Finns sent representatives to the election of kings, and soldiers to fight in Sweden's foreign wars.

During the Kalmar Union of 1397–1523, a series of chance dynastic coincidences and deals led the countries of Scandinavia to bond together under a single ruler. Denmark, Norway and Sweden became a single realm, with Finland, as Sweden's easternmost marches, also included. The union, however, also caused the administrative capital to move from Stockholm to Copenhagen, leaving the Finns further on the periphery. This isolation was accentuated during the Black Death, which killed off a third of the population of all Sweden, including the vulnerable homesteads of the remote Eastland. According to one eerie folktale everybody in the township of Espoo died except for a girl and a monk. When the monk, too, succumbed, the girl climbed the church tower and tolled the bell in his memory, signalling her presence to the only other survivor in the vicinity, her future husband. Like an Adam and Eve of the borderlands, the couple became the ancestors of many future residents of Espoo, although much of the repopulation was arranged through royal decree, with boatloads of new settlers sent from the motherland.

After the break-up of the Kalmar Union, Finland became more prominent once more, as the Eastland of a Greater Sweden, which, at its height, straddled not only the north shores of the Baltic, but also extended south into what is now Estonia and Lithuania. This, in turn, involved the Finns indirectly in Sweden's many wars, as the master of the Baltic continued to jostle for influence against the Danes, the Russians and the rising power of Germany.

The Pähkinäsaari line was often ignored. Despite the promise not to build castles along it, the Swedes put up several (see Gazetteer: Savonlinna). An entire community of trappers and hunters, the *Pirkkalaiset*, named for their original settlement in Pirkkala near Tampere, gained the right from the Swedish crown to fish in Lapland and collect tax from the locals – so the pacification of the borderlands was essentially farmed out to private industry, and woe betide any Russians who might run into them.

Meanwhile, a minor issue of religion would prove to have lasting implications, when the dioceses of Uppsala and Turku established the line that marked the edges of their authority at Tornio, establishing a precedent for the boundary between 'Finland' and the rest of Sweden. Finland itself acquired greater influence during the 15th century, where its position as a marchland made it a crucible for forging future leaders.

Eric of Pomerania, King of all Scandinavia in the early 1400s, had spent his youth as the overlord of the Finnish border regions. Finland was a land with plenty of castles, and castles meant noblemen with armed retinues that needed to be appeased – turning many Finnish governors into members of the councils and king-making power blocs. In 1448, the Lord of Vyborg castle and former Lord of Turku was himself elected king, taking the throne as King Karl VIII (the first of three occasions, owing to the usual squabbling and politicking among the nobles of the time).

In 1523, the Reformation reached Finland in the figure of King Gustav I Vasa, who would see Catholicism ousted in his reign as Sweden's state religion, replaced by Lutheranism. This in turn would have far-reaching consequences, not the least the translation of the Bible into Finnish by Mikael Agricola. Along with the same author's more modest but more immediately useful *ABC-kirja*, this not only taught Finns to read and write, but established the foundations of Finnish as a recognised language, and Finnishness as something separate from Sweden.

'Finlande is called a fayre Countrye, because it is more pleasanter than Swecia,' wrote George North in 1561, thereby making himself a hero evermore in the Finn-Swede standoff.

> Muche wyne is transported thither; out of Spayne, by the sea Balthic, which the people of the Country much desyreth, onely to exhillerat their myndes ... The Finnons have continual warres with the Muscouites in the arme or bosome of the sea Finnonicus: usyng in Summer the ayde of Shyppes, and in Wynter they combat upon the Ise.

According to popular lore in Europe, Finns were not only drunk, they were drunken wizards. Olaus Magnus, in his *Description of the Northern Peoples* in 1555, notes that there once was a time when:

> Finns, among other pagan delusions, would offer wind for sale to traders who were detained on their coasts by off-shore gales, and when payment had been brought would give them in return three magic knots tied in a strap not likely to break.

Untying the first knot would supposedly rustle up a gentle breeze. The second would bring gusts sufficient to fill the sails of any ship. But the third would unleash hellish gales more likely to wreck the vessel than take it to a safe harbour.

Olaus is swift to pour scorn on the very idea, offering an enlightened and curiously modern rant about gullible people's willingness to read rational outcomes into irrational claims. But the inhabitants of Lapland were clearly regarded even into the 16th century as a people with magical powers. Olaus devotes several scornful chapters to the 'witches and wizards of the Finns,' and when Shakespeare wishes to conjure up an image of bewitched confusion in *The Comedy of Errors* (c.1594), he notes: 'Lapland sorcerers inhabit here.'

However, such authors' willingness to identify the people of the Arctic region as magicians owed something to their era. Both Olaus Magnus and Shakespeare were writing at a time when Lapland truly was the last frontier of European paganism. Although there had been earlier, sporadic exercises in preaching and conversion, missionaries only really arrived in force in the 17th and 18th centuries. With Christianity, of course, came a deep mistrust of pagan beliefs and ways of living – the purges and witch trials of the era saw the trampling of many folk traditions of medicine and belief. One of the most damaging acts of the missionaries in Lapland was the confiscation of shamanic drums from the priests of the Saami. The seat of a *noaidi* shaman's power, such drum-skins seem to have contained numerous mnemonic devices, symbolic summaries of rituals, and possibly even planisphere-like images of the constellations overhead. Pitifully few originals survive today, particularly since a misunderstanding over the missionaries' interest in the drums led to the manufacture of hundreds of fakes. During a period when earnest missionaries agreed to pay a small amnesty fee for any drums handed over, Saami in outlying regions commenced a cottage industry churning out new drums to exchange for cash. As a result, there is still some doubt as to the true provenance even of those supposedly genuine drums that can be found in Finnish museums.

Finland in the Northern Wars

By 1617, Lapland had been officially incorporated within the Swedish realm, after the treaty of Stolbova ended the seven-year Ingrian War, in which the Swedes had, as ever, attempted to push their borders further east. Sweden's 'Age of Greatness' included further wars over mastery of the Baltic, not only against Denmark, but also against the newly rising power of Poland, and ultimately in the Thirty Years War that engulfed almost all of the countries of Europe.

The 'Swedish' army in Europe included three regiments of light cavalry from Finland, from the Hämeenlinna, Turku and Viipuri regions. They fought in many battles of the 1630s and 1640s, and were often known as the Hakkapeliitta, from their battle cry of *Hakkaa päälle!* ('Cut them down!' or more literally 'Strike on!'). To hear the Finns talk about them, you might be forgiven for thinking they were world-famous, but this seems to be a story that the Finns tell themselves, popularised by the works of Topelius (see Chapter 3), and reinforced in countless attempts by 19th-century schoolteachers to interest their classes in the complexities of the Thirty Years War. It was Topelius, in search of stirring narratives of the Finnish past, who popularised the 'Hakkapeliitta March' by translating the war-song of the 17th-century riders into Swedish. It remains on the repertoire of military bands in Sweden, Finland and Germany, even though several of its verses amount to little more than bragging about places the singers have despoiled, and people they've killed. The verses that sound slightly less like a party of rappers celebrating a drive-by shooting read as follows:

The snowy north is our fatherland;
There our hearth crackles on the stormy beach.
There our sinewy arm grew by the sword,
There our chests burned with faith and honour.

[...]

Take heart, you who dwell in darkness and chains!
We're coming, we're coming, we will free your hand.
Slaves do not sigh in our frosty North;
Freeborn we ride into the field for God's word.

[...]

And if we ride far from our northern track,
To glowing grenades and bleeding wounds,

Then the trumpets call the message of our victory.
Cut them down, brave ranks! Forward! With us is God.

The 'Hakkapeliitta March' sounds oddly old-fashioned in the Finnish musical repertoire. Its tune is musically uninspiring; it is dwarfed and overshadowed by the stirring efforts of later composers like Sibelius. But the lyrics are nice enough, and the attention paid to them by Finnish educators has helped obscure the likelihood that nobody in Europe who heard the song ever actually understood the words, sung as they were in impenetrable Finnish.

Nor were the allies of the Hakkapeliitta all that sure who they were. One story of the Thirty Years War mentions a parade of soldiers, led by brightly-attired mercenaries and hired swords, companies distinguished by flashes of regimental blue, or yellow or green. Bringing up the rear were nondescript cavalrymen on their small, shaggy, fierce-looking ponies, with no notable uniform or brigade symbol, their trousers held up with string, and their horses bridled with chunks of birch-bark, their cutlasses dragging on the ground as if forgotten, their eyes stern and their cheeks hollowed.

The baffled Dutch ambassador asked what he was looking at, only for a German quartermaster to say he was looking at the Life Guards regiment. He then shouted '*Perkele!*' which he seems to have thought was their battle-cry, or possibly their regimental cheer. In fact, it is a Finnish swear-word, presumably the only identifiable bit of Finnish he had ever heard from them, tantamount to the modern-day French observers who assumed that British football hooligans are called *les fuckoffs*.

The many wars and conflicts of the era found the Swedes jostling once more for supremacy in the Baltic, particularly against an even stronger Russia, as Novgorod was now absorbed within the larger princedom of Muscovy. Sweden met its match in the disastrous Battle of Poltava, in 1709 in what is now Ukraine. King Karl XII escaped, but spent the next five years in Moldavia, then part of the Ottoman Empire, pleading with his allies to lend him the money for a rematch. He would eventually return, bringing with him designs for two Ottoman-inspired warships, some new recipes (see Chapter 7: Eating and Drinking), and even some new vocabulary – a Swedish term for a disturbance, *kalabalik*, derives from the Turkish for 'crowd,' referring to the mobs of angry locals who descended on the growing camp of Swedish refugees.

In his absence, Finland suffered the years of the Great Wrath – occupation by the soldiers of Tsar Peter the Great. Thousands were killed, thousands more taken away as slaves, and a brutal scorched-earth policy pursued in order to create a barrier against Swedish counter-attacks. The Russians were gone by 1721, but only after the signature of the Treaty of Uusikaupunki, which cost Sweden much of the lands near Vyborg, and all its territory in and around Estonia. The change marked the end of Sweden's age as a great power, and the beginning of Russia's, while much of the damage was done, as usual, in Finland.

Sweden attempted to regain Vyborg in 1741, in a fool-hardily intricate scheme that was supposed to distract other countries from coups and skulduggery, but ended only with another defeat at the hands of the Russians. With the Swedish fleet paralysed by an epidemic of disease and unable to lend naval support to the attack, the Russians went on a swift counter-offensive, occupying Finland yet again in what is known as the Lesser Wrath. A treaty signed in Turku in 1743 would cost Sweden yet more territory, with the area around Lappeenranta and Hamina also handed to Russia.

With every treaty merely a temporary hiatus in hostilities, the Swedes prepared for another conflict, fortifying an island off the shore at Helsinki in the hope of making the city impregnable. The construction of this Fortress of the Swedes (*Sveaborg*), better known today as the Fortress of Finland

(*Suomenlinna*) was witnessed in the 1780s by William Coxe, an English clergyman.

> The works are really stupendous and worthy of the ancient Romans. The walls are chiefly of hewn granite, covered with earth, from six to ten feet thick, and in a few places not less than 48 in height. The batteries, which begin upon a level with the water, and rise in tiers one above the other in all directions, commanding the only channel through which large vessels can sail to Helsingfors, render the passage of an enemy's fleet extremely dangerous, if not impracticable.

Despite all these awe-inspiring preparations, the fortress would not help. The final blow came in 1808, with a 19-month conflict between Sweden and Russia that would come to be known as the Finnish War, because Finland was the prize. Mired in the posturings and alliances of the Napoleonic conflict, it led to a Russian invasion of Finland without an official declaration of war, and the complete occupation of Finnish territory by winter 1808. In 1809, the nobles of Finland officially accepted that they had a new ruler, one who would hopefully not involve them in quite so many foreign wars. The Swedish era was over, with Finland's acceptance of the Russian Tsar Alexander I as its new head of state.

The Swedish Legacy

Linguistic evidence of the Swedish era endures in Finland, in everything from bilingual street signs to twinned subtitles in movie theatres. Finland's entire northern shoreline is named Ostrobothnia – which is to say, it is described as the *east* coast of the gulf of Bothnia, rather than 'west' Finland. South-west Finland, the rump around Turku, is still called Varsinais-Suomi ('Finland Proper'), a relic of the late medieval period when Swedish authority only really extended around the reach of Turku castle. A little north of there is Satakunta ('The Hundred'), an indicator of the slow extension of farms and authority.

The long stretch of southern coast from Turku to Helsinki is still called Uusimaa ('New Land'), a direct calque of the original Swedish *Nyland*, which was named for its status as a colony by royal decree. Helsinki itself takes its name originally from Hälsingland, the region in central Sweden from which many colonists were sent to populate the new trade route towards Russia. And more immediately and importantly, all Finns still have to learn Swedish at school. Swedish remains one of the country's two official languages, and is still the mother tongue of some 265,000 Finns (5% of the country). These are largely concentrated on the west and south coasts, historically the most 'Swedish' areas, where one can still often find street signs written in Swedish first and then Finnish. In particular, the Åland Islands, halfway between Finland and Sweden, are a Finnish possession but entirely Swedish-speaking.

This linguistic relic is often more visible to the tourist than to the resident, as any encounter with artefacts and figures from before the 19th century is sure to be heavily Swedish in nature – inscriptions, names and fashions. There are statues of Swedish kings in the town centres of the Ostrobothnian coast, the food is often obviously Swedish in nature, and YLE Fem, the country's fifth TV channel, broadcasts in Swedish.

Of course, allegiance and connections to Sweden also signified a degree of wealth and standing, such that Swedish speakers formed all but three of Finland's noble families. Although modern Finland is bluntly, sometimes defensively egalitarian, any baron or count encountered in the history books is liable to be a Swedish-speaker. Swedish remained the default language of administration, the military and education up until the later 19th century, in turn ensuring that anyone with a desire to truly understand the history of

Finland must also learn Swedish. As late as 1894, Senator George Forsman caused gasps and uproar when he chose to address the Estate of Nobility in Finnish, instead of the Swedish lingua franca.

Wealth creates free time, and free time brings the greater likelihood of a career in the arts. This, in turn, favoured a Swedish-speaking bias among many of Finland's most famous creatives, including artists and writers before the 19th century, when Finnish nationalism began to assert itself in radical, vibrant, enduring ways. With the Finnish language still struggling to develop modes and metres, clichés and archetypes, many of the coming decades' assertions of Finn-ishness would be written first in Swedish.

But as the Finns were once ghosts in Sweden, the Swedes have become ghosts in Finland – a palpable presence along the west and south, but fading fast in the hinterland. You will hear their language in announcements on the train and bus; you will catch their weather forecasts; you will see tips of the hat to them in everything from street signs to flags, but they continue to dwindle, like the echoes of a lost age.

3

The Russian Century: 1809–1899

SENAATINTORI (SENATE SQUARE) sits in the very heart of imperial Helsinki, overlooking the harbour and its island fortress of Suomenlinna. It is flanked on all sides by institutions of authority – the great, classical columns of Helsinki Cathedral atop the steps on its north side; and the serried bookshelves of Helsinki University's main building on its west. On the eastern side is the former senate building, which now houses the Finnish prime minister and his or her staff. On the south side is Sederholm House, the oldest mansion in Helsinki.

In its centre stands a statue of a bushy-moustached man in the bulky epaulets and frog-tied tunic of a 19th-century general. But he stands at ease, his weight nonchalantly on his back foot, his right palm extended in a conciliatory fashion, as if he is making a friendly suggestion to an unseen audience. At his feet lurk a group of symbolic classical goddesses: Iustitia (Justice), wearing the pelt of a lion; Pax (Peace) with her customary doves; and Lux (Light/Enlightenment), bearing a scientific instrument and accompanied by a lyre-playing cherub. With them are a gaggle of tough-looking peasants, representing honest labour.

The man who presides over this menagerie is Alexander II (1818–1881), the 'Good Tsar,' a figure loved so much by the Finns that his statue has endured in the centre of

Helsinki throughout the Revolution, the conflicts of the 20th century, Stalinism and the Cold War. He is captured here in a moment from 1863, in the act of re-convening the Diet of Finland, that body of local government that had not met since its leading noblemen had pledged their allegiance to their new Russian masters in 1809. Seemingly using the underpopulated Finland as an experimental test subject for potential reforms elsewhere in his empire, Alexander II bestowed upon it an element of home rule, its own currency (the *markka*, pegged initially as a quarter of the value of the Russian rouble), and a relaxation of the rules on using Russian in public institutions and records.

The statue is a glimpse of another bygone age – many modern Finns have grown up in a realm fiercely suspicious of Russia and Russians, and seem to have an ideological blind spot when it comes to the Tsar in the middle of their capital. But even after Alexander II's death, he remained a popular figure with the Finns, particularly as his heirs squandered his achievements. Throughout the reigns of his son, Alexander III and ill-fated grandson, Nicholas II, the base of the statue would often be garlanded with flowers by reverent Finns. As the political climate turned increasingly frosty, Finns turned to the only means of subtle protest left to them, demonstrating their loyalty to Russia by honouring its ruler, but choosing to honour the ruler they loved the best, rather than his ham-fisted successors.

Even today, one sometimes finds flowers at the base of the statue, mourning a Russian love affair long turned sour.

THE RUSSIANS WERE WELL AWARE that the people of the newly occupied territory occasionally chafed against the Swedes. The occupation hence began with a careful series of proclamations aimed at suggesting to the Finns that Russian suzerainty was really a better deal than remaining subjects of the Swedes. The Diet, it was claimed (misleadingly), would still be convened. The Finns were free to practice their Lutheran faith, and the noble estates would be preserved.

The message, then, was business as usual, with assurances of some degree of political autonomy, religious freedom and no requisition of people's wealth. Many Finns greeted the news with little more than a shrug at the exchange of one unseen ruler for another.

'A defenceless country is like the sea,' commented one bishop pragmatically. 'Who is there to call it a sin if its waves roll up the shore the wind has driven them to? God has given us a ruler, and we must hold him up in honour.'

Russian troops were still skirmishing with Swedes elsewhere when the Tsar convened the Diet in Porvoo, March 1809. There, the nobility, as representatives of all Finns, swore allegiance to the Tsar, who whipped up a frenzy of unlikely hopes by commenting in his speech that the Finns had now been 'elevated to the family of nations.'

Timing was everything. Because the Finns had volunteered to accept Russian suzerainty before the Swedes had concluded peace, Finland's status was substantially higher than it might have been mere weeks later. Finland was never a conquered *province* of Russia, but instead an annexed Grand Duchy – the Tsar becoming its princely head of state.

The Russians were not particularly impressed with Finland. Since they already had trees, lakes and snow of their own, the country initially had little to offer but a buffer zone between them and the rest of Europe, with limited transport and amenities, and thousands of square miles of wilderness and forest, stretching all the way to the Arctic.

'Boredom crawls over the snow wastes,' moaned the soldier Konstantin Batyushkov in 1809, 'and one can truly say that life in this wild barren solitude, without books, without company and often without aquavit is so miserable that we cannot tell whether it is Wednesday or Sunday.'

The French exile Madame de Staël was similarly dismissive on passing through in 1812, noting: 'They try to cultivate the mind a little there, but bears and wolves come so close in winter that all thought is of necessity concentrated on how to obtain a tolerable physical existence.'

By 1833, the prevailing opinion had changed little, with the poet Alexander Pushkin pronouncing Finland to be 'Nature's unhappy stepson', seemingly dealt all the pain of outdoors life, but with none of its pleasures. But Alexander II's reforms came accompanied by greater freedoms on foreign investment, and a new programme of railway-building that locked Finland closer to the Russian metropolis of St Petersburg. It should be said that this was much more important for the Finns than for the Russians, who had a whole empire to fret about, including ever-advancing tracts of nation-sized land in the Siberian east. Consequently, despite the prominent position of Alexander II in Finnish history, Finland itself hardly gets a mention in Edvard Radzinsky's biography of the Tsar, barely warranting two index entries in a 450-page book.

Industrial Revolutions

The Russian era came accompanied by coincidental changes in technology and economy that were largely to the Finns' benefit. The industrial revolution elsewhere in Europe created an unexpected demand for Finnish wood and tar, which turned up as far afield as Britain, shoring up the roofs of coal pits and caulking ships of the line. Several British firms invested directly in Finnish lumber businesses, in order to ensure a steady supply. This in turn contributed to a rationalisation of water transport, with many of the scattered lakes linked by new canals. By 1856, it was possible to steam in a ship all the way from Viipuri on the Baltic coast to Kuopio, some 300 kilometres inland to the north.

Meanwhile, the exponential rise all over Europe of mass literacy and newsprint created a boom in the demand for paper, pouring money into the Finnish economy. Railways began arriving in the 1860s, with the early lines of the Finnish network connecting directly to St Petersburg in 1870. Although Finland had (and still has) remarkably few railway lines, those that it has have connected inland industrial areas to the sea ports since the late 19th century.

The Scottish missionary John Paterson spent much of the early 18th century in the Nordic countries, and was intimately involved in the translation of the Bible into many local languages (oddly, since the Bible had been available in Finnish for centuries). He was particularly taken with the rapids at Tampere, and inadvertently evangelised on the town's behalf. His posthumously-published memoirs *The Book for Every Land* (1858) recount what happened when Paterson finally brought his friend James Finlayson face-to-face with the churning waters. Finlayson was less interested in natural beauty than in the implications of a 20-metre drop in water height for setting up a mill.

> My friend Finlayson was delighted with the place. He at once perceived that I had not over-rated it in my description to him ... On our return to Petersburg, Mr Finlayson applied to Government for the grant of a small piece of land, on which to erect a manufactory for spinning cotton, and other purposes, and a sufficient command of water for the purpose. All and more than he asked was granted; and here works have been erected, which employ some hundreds of poor people, and being now entirely in the hands of pious men ... are a great blessing to the country ...

Although Finlayson had sold up by 1836, his name became synonymous with the six-storey factory he founded, the first in Finland to install electric lighting, and a power-house of the Industrial Revolution that led to Tampere's odd nickname, 'the Manchester of Finland' (see Gazetteer: Tampere). Although Finland produced no raw cotton of its own, Alexander II's promise not to impose duty on

Finlayson's imported materials remained good for the rest of the 19th century, and allowed the mills to become a centre for employment and development.

Steam tugs on the canals brought Russian tourists deeper into the lake land, but steam ships on the Baltic cut Finland off from many previous visitors. In the 18th century, many European travellers had regarded Finland as a necessary stop on the way to St Petersburg, making landfall at Turku and traversing the long coastal road along the Gulf of Finland. However, by the 19th century, steamship technology allowed any traveller in a hurry to board a vessel taking them straight to their destination, deleting Finland from many travellers' itineraries, but also ensuring that anyone who did go there was intent on enjoying it for its own sake, and not as something to stare at from the window of a post carriage. Finland became a place associated in the tourist's mind with wilderness and exotic Nordic open spaces, as best summed up by Ethel Brilliana 'Mrs Alec' Tweedie, the Victorian traveller whose journey around the country in the 1890s, *Through Finland in Carts*, remains an enchanting snapshot, both of Finns and of foreigners' perceptions of them.

> No one ever dreamed of going to Finland. Nevertheless, Finland is not the home of barbarians, as some folk then imagined; neither do Polar bears walk continually about the streets, nor reindeer pull sledges in summer – items that have several times been suggested to the writer.

Few Finns noticed that the Tsar's reforms also lured them further away from their former masters in Sweden, encouraging trade links and travel to the east, rather than the west. Finns eventually became renowned as some of the most loyal and agreeable subjects of the Russian Empire, particularly in St Petersburg, where Finnish serving girls and sailors were common sights in the houses and taverns.

The same industrial revolution that put steamships into the Baltic also put smog into St Petersburg and anger into the hearts of the Russian working class. Travel restrictions on Tsarist Russians, designed to stop them learning unhelpful ideas like democracy and liberalism, led many of them to take their vacations in the only 'foreign' country within Russian authority, turning Finland's southern coast and eastern lakes into a vast Riviera of spa resorts and rural *dachas*. In particular, Terijoki (see The Lost Lands: Zelenogorsk) became a veritable St Petersburg-on-sea, a bracing seaside resort for Russian holidaymakers, and notorious for occasional seafront brawls between drunken tourists. For the later Tsars, after the tragic assassination of Alexander II by Russian anarchists in 1881, Finland became a popular holiday destination because it was *not* Russia, and Finns could usually be counted on not to blow them up or shoot them while they were fishing or sunning themselves.

Laestadius & Laestadianism

Guarantees of religious freedom allowed the Protestant Lutherans to co-exist alongside the Eastern Orthodox Russians. Up in Lapland, the descendants of the Saami were facing increasing restrictions on their way of life. The Swedish placards of the late 17th century had not been reversed under Russian rule, leading to ever-encroaching homesteads and claims on what had once been deemed wilderness. Divisions and enclosures of land played havoc with Saami territorial concepts, particularly since many Saami tended to think in terms of access to *water*, rather than to the land around it. In an impasse bleakly familiar among many native peoples, the Saami were found to be in a long and precipitous decline into alcoholism and depression.

Lars Levi Laestadius (1800–1861) was a pastor born into a Saami family in what was at least officially Swedish Lapland. Despite being of Saami ethnicity, and devoted to the cause of improving the conditions of his countrymen, he was also a super-devout Christian, determined not only to rescue the Saami from alcoholism, but to prevent them doing the Devil's work by whistling or calling to their reindeer with *joiks* (songs).

Laestadius got his first parish posting in his late twenties, and spent the next 20 years preaching the Gospel and administering to his flock in Karesuando – still technically in Sweden, but right on the Finnish border, on the 'wrist' of the map's Maid of Finland, and where the common tongue among the disparate herders and town-dwellers was Finnish. He fathered 12 children with his Saami wife, and functioned as a guide and botanist on a French academic expedition across Lapland, which would eventually result in his *Fragments of Lappish Mythology*, invaluable today as one of the only surviving accounts of the local folklore he was intent on stamping out.

In 1844, he first encountered a revivalist movement among the Saami that distinguished between true believers and 'false Christians'. Drawn by its fundamentalist principles and its inclusive, egalitarian practice that effectively rendered all true believers to be priests, able to hear confession from others, Laestadius fast became the leading light of the splinter group, which eventually took his name. He eventually died in 1861, leaving his name nestled in the Latin designations of several Scandinavian plants, a temperance movement that would continue to grow throughout the latter part of the 19th century, and an Apostolic Lutheran sect that endures in isolated pockets in Finland, Scandinavia and those parts of the USA with a substantial population of Fenno-Scandinavian immigrants.

The most conservative of today's Laestadians, like the grimmest of Lutherans, Adventists and similar revivalist denominations, continue to refer to themselves as 'true' believers, with the implication that everybody else is worshipping graven idols. Their services, as in the time of Laestadius, are lively and vibrant affairs, complete with sinners begging their fellows for forgiveness. Of the world's 115,000 conservative Laestadians (the splinter group having further splintered) most are to be found in modern Finland where their existence is unlikely to reach the notice of the average tourist. Their presence, however, becomes decidedly more palpable for anyone who has raised a child in Finland, as Laestadian families tend to be noticeable at daycare and schools. Shunning contraception, they tend to the larger size, particularly when their insistence of no sex before marriage incentivises couples to get married as soon as possible. Hence, it is not unusual to run into a married couple in their late twenties with five children, nourished and well-kept by the Finnish education system, and often impeccably well behaved, thanks to the Laestadians' hatred of television and cinemas. This latter proscription, however, is being eroded in many Laestadian homes, as rules-lawyers insist that the internet 'doesn't count' as TV, and therefore everyone can huddle around the computer to watch the latest sinful episode of *The Amazing Race*.

The Åland War

In 1853 the outbreak of the Crimean War pitted the Tsar's Russian Empire, including the Grand Duchy of Finland, against an international coalition including the fading might of the Ottoman Empire, shored up by its British and French allies. Much of the fighting, of course, was in Crimea itself, but the conflict also led to skirmishes as far afield as Kamchatka and Sardinia. Much overlooked in histories of the Crimean War is the two-year campaign in the Baltic Sea, where an Anglo-French taskforce shelled the edges of the Russian Empire, and bottled the Tsar's fleet in St Petersburg. Most crucially, the Tsar's constant fear of an attack on St Petersburg itself led him to keep 30,000 Russian soldiers stationed close at hand, thereby keeping them away from the main theatre.

Despite this contribution, the actions of the British in the Baltic have been largely forgotten. Admirals get famous for *sinking* ships, not simply keeping their enemy distracted and setting fire to the tar silos. Moreover, the Baltic action was also something of an embarrassment, since on several occasions attempted British landings were thwarted by simple geographical hazards and a population of bullish locals. At least one Finnish coastal town still talks proudly of the dead English sailors in its graveyard, and has yet to return the gunboat that unwisely attacked it (see Gazetteer: Kokkola).

The allies' greatest success was the destruction of Bomarsund, a recently constructed Russian sea-fort overlooking the strategic harbour in the middle of the Åland Islands (see Gazetteer: Ahvenanmaa). Less successful were several assaults on Helsinki's off-shore fortress Sveaborg (better known today by its Finnish name, Suomenlinna), the cause of much finger-pointing. The admiral on site was convinced that Sveaborg was unassailable without a particular kind of low-draft mortar-launcher that he lacked; armchair generals back home were equally sure that he simply lacked the courage or intelligence to carry out his orders.

The worst long-term effect of the Baltic campaign was the damage to the reputation of the 'English' among the Finns, who had long cherished the notion of a special affinity with the nation that had, after all, supplied their patron saint. This was not lost even back in Britain, where questions were asked in Parliament about the wisdom of carrying out a war against Russia by attacking defenceless Finnish villagers, and burning the tar warehouses of Oulu and Raahe.

More than 150 years after the Baltic campaign, it is still a recurring museum feature all along the coast of Finland, where despite the modern might of the steam navy, the skerries and shallows often reduced the attackers' presence to humble rowboats and landing parties that were considerably more vulnerable than the warships that launched them.

A song, purportedly celebrating the defence of the Åland Islands, has entered the modern Finnish military repertoire, despite its best-known version's careful avoidance of mentioning that the Finns actually surrendered. Here is part of it:

Oh the Åland War was horrific
Hurrah! Hurrah! Hurrah!
When on three hundred ships
Came the Englishmen sailing to our Finnish coast
Sunfaraa Sunfaraa Sunfaralalala
Hurrah! Hurrah! Hurrah!

[...]

But the Finnish boys fired at them
Hurrah! Hurrah! Hurrah!
Echoing round the walls of the island fastness
Ringing on the Åland shores
Sunfaraa Sunfaraa Sunfaralalala
Hurrah! Hurrah! Hurrah!

'Oolannin Sota' (the Åland War) is a stirring toe-tapper, sure to be dragged out at military occasions, which, in a country that still has national service, is liable to involve almost everybody's family at some point in their lives. It also seems particularly popular with Finnish maiden aunts who wish to torment British authors by singing it constantly to their half-Finnish children while babysitting – many are the times, when writing this book, that your correspondent has been assailed by *Hurrahs* from downstairs.

The problem with 'Oolannin Sota' is that it appears to have sprung up out of nowhere; it is entirely unknown on the Åland Islands themselves, where the claim that the local beaches amounted to 'our Finnish coast' would be regarded by many of the Swedish-speaking locals as somewhat provocative.

It was included in an early book of Finnish military music in 1918, but no song with that title pre-dating 1910 has been unearthed. As one might expect from a song purported to come from the Åland Islands, the language of the song is heavily peppered with actual Swedish words, although the first extant version of it in Swedish is a translation from what appears to be the 'original' Finnish.

It was not until 1975 that a musicologist found a 19th-century edition of the similarly named 'Ålandin Sota', a close match in melodic terms, but with substantially different words. While the version most widely known and sung is an exuberant, triumphal celebration of the brave Finns repulsing the hapless Englishmen, the song uncovered by Kalevi Ijäs in a remote mainland farm is a far more honest account of the destruction of Bomarsund. It appears that the original version of 'Ålandin Sota' may have been written by one Johan Wallenius, a Finnish prisoner of war from Bomarsund, who sat out the last months of the conflict along with several hundred other Finns in the East Sussex town of Lewes.

The 'Russian' prisoners of war in Lewes are commemorated by a stone obelisk that still stands in the local churchyard of St John sub Castro. Commissioned by Tsar Alexander II, the memorial records the names of 28 'Russians' who died during their incarceration – the names are almost universally those of Finnish conscripts, rather than their Russian officers. Their surviving fellow inmates became local celebrities in the town, regarded as exotic foreign curios, and put to work on what proved to be a lucrative carpentry business making 'Russian' toys for sale to local children.

It seems that while languishing in relative luxury in Lewes' Old Gaol, the prisoners wrote the original version of the song, quite possibly adding new verses as their own story went on, resulting in a version much longer than the one sung today, with 18 verses penned in an odd patois of half-remembered Swedish and misspelt Finnish – as if illiterate Ostrobothnian farmboys were attempting to remember officers' terms they had never correctly heard in the first place.

Their account tells of the war coming to the Ålands, and of the 'Finnish boys' shipped over from the mainland to prepare for their defence. 'Two hundred' ships arrive in this version, crewed with greater historical accuracy by both French and Englishmen (the terms mangled almost childishly into *franskalaine* and *engetesman*). There is an attack, there is a command given in haste, and then some accusatory verses about the unnecessary deaths this causes. The 'flag of grace' is raised in surrender, and the Finnish boys are marched away to an uncertain fate. They live for 'a year and eight months in the English kingdom' before being allowed to return home.

> Then came the command from the Emperor
> *Hurrah! Hurrah! Hurrah!*
> That allows the captured boys and their father back to
>   their land.
> *Sunka fralla* [seemingly a mangled version of the
>   Swedish for 'Sing tralala']
>
> So the boys they cheered and shouted
> *Hurrah! Hurrah! Hurrah!*
> And said their farewells through the town of Leves [sic],
> As they stepped down to their white/fire ship
> *Sunka fralla*
>
> And the boys sang in the harbour
> *Hurrah! Hurrah! Hurrah!*
> That the English kingdom was wonderful
> But our fatherland is yet more marvellous
> *Sunka fralla*

Translating even the basic sense of it is difficult, when one can see that the authors meant one word, but only because they had misheard another. There may have even been multiple versions of a collectively-written song, diverging into one form in which the Finns return home in a *valki-alaiva* (strangely poetic, but presumably a steam ship), and another in which the Finns leave in a *tulivaunu* (a 'chariot of fire', possibly referring to the 28 prisoners who died, or possibly a sweetly clueless reference to a steam train). It remains an odd, indistinct echo of real lives catapulted from the shores of Finland to the English coast, and home again, one-and-a-half centuries ago.

The *Kalevala*

It was during the Russian century that Elias Lönnrot (1802–1884), a physician and folklorist, collected a different sort of song in the wilds of Karelia. Posted to the remote town of Kajaani for much of his career, Lönnrot busied himself by taking prolonged journeys into the eastern lands, collecting and collating songs and stories from local story-tellers.

His aim, among the peasants of the remote communities, was to dig up specifically Finnish folktales that might have endured in the hinterland even as they were wiped out by the onslaught of Swedish and Russian culture in the towns. Adding bridging material of his own, Lönnrot fashioned the disparate stories into a single song-cycle, publishing it as the *Kalevala*, Finland's national epic.

The cycle of stories, as eventually set down by Lönnrot, presents a creation myth and series of epic conflicts among the forests and lakes of an ancient Finland. It remains charmingly modest in its aspirations, and its depiction of a relatively simple life in the forests – it has no fairytale castles, and the ancient gods of Finland take a back seat. Instead, it is preoccupied with the bickering and feuds of a bunch of heroes, rich with detail about daily life and material culture in the Finnish Dark Ages – enough material, in fact, to function as a blueprint for an entire immersive re-enactment experience in modern times (see Gazetteer: Kuhmo).

Although the gods are occasionally present, the stories of the *Kalevala* dwell for most of the time on the heroes, particularly 'steadfast, old Väinämöinen', the first man. We see him born to the goddess Ilmatar, and instrumental in the creation of many elements of the Finnish natural world and ancient society.

Väinämöinen is already an old man when he encounters and duels with the hero Joukahainen, who promises him his sister Aino as a bride if he spares his life. Väinämöinen agrees, only for Aino to drown herself in a lake. Several stories then follow in which these heroes are presented as long-suffering woodsmen, toiling in a series of herculean labours in the hope of winning the hand of another fair maiden. In particular, several heroes chase after the daughters of Louhi, the shape-shifting queen of the northern land of Pohjola. Väinämöinen persuades the master-smith Ilmarinen to create the Sampo, a magical device of indeterminate function that may have once been a magical shield, or icon or symbol. Lönnrot's version suggests it is a machine or cornucopia, part forge and part mill.

> On one side the flour is grinding,
> On another salt is making,
> On a third is money forging,
> And the lid is many-colored.
> Well the Sampo grinds when finished,
> To and fro the lid in rocking,
> Grinds one measure at the day-break,
> Grinds a measure fit for eating,
> Grinds a second for the market,
> Grinds a third one for the store-house.

Whatever it is, and much ink has been spilled over it ever since, it soon turns into a MacGuffin over which everybody is fighting. Louhi sets a number of impossible tasks for the heroes who want to marry her daughters. The hero

Lemminkäinen dies attempting such missions, but is raised from the dead by his sorcerous mother. Ilmarinen the smith actually completes his tasks, with the help of the Maiden of the North, who is clearly sweet on him. The result is the wedding to end all weddings, in which heroic guests provide ostentatious gifts and food, and there is much celebration, all except for Lemminkäinen, who is not invited, and stomps off sulkily to have a series of adventures on his own.

But there is no happy-ever-after for Ilmarinen and his new wife. She picks on the wrong slave, a troubled orphan called Kullervo, whose difficult early life forms a separate, ominous story cycle, not unlike a flashback in which someone discovers that the person whose seat he just stole on the train is actually Hannibal Lecter. Kullervo sees his mistress dead at the claws of a gang of wolves and bears, and then runs off to avenge his family, starting a war and inadvertently having sex with his sister, before killing himself in grief.

Single once more, Ilmarinen attempts to make himself a woman out of gold and silver, but finds her unsurprisingly emotionless. Instead, he heads off back to the north to snatch another of Louhi's daughters, leaving in a hurry after having turned the angry Louhi into a bird. Back in the south, he tells Väinämöinen of the wealth that the Sampo has brought to Louhi's people, and the heroes head off to steal it. In the massive, sorcerous apocalypse that follows, armies of men are slaughtered on both sides, as the combatants war with steel, ships and magical songs. The Sampo falls into the ocean while set in its condiment mode, and is still somewhere at the bottom, endlessly churning out salt. The vengeful Louhi orders a series of plagues on the south, and the heroes fight back with a prolonged series of magical solutions and damage controls.

Finally, almost as an afterthought, a virgin called Marjatta gives birth to a baby boy (see Chapter 1), having become pregnant by eating a berry. Väinämöinen orders it to be killed, but the child scolds him and is baptised as the King of

Karelia. Realising that the time of the old beliefs has passed, Väinämöinen leaves his realm in the hands of the Christ-figure, and sails away.

National Romanticism

The *Kalevala*'s impact was immense. Among European literati, it became a subject of great debate, since Lönnrot had seemingly uncovered an epic worthy of comparison to Greek and Roman classics among illiterate peasants at the edge of the known world. It was also seized upon as a work of inspiring nationalism, arguing, in the fashion of the Brothers Grimm, that a people who had a story and a language also had the right to a nation. As a truly *national* myth, divorced from associations with either Sweden or Russia, the *Kalevala* was also seized upon by a generation of Finnish artists in search of 'Finnish' subjects.

Aleksis Kivi (1834–1872) chose the *Kalevala* as the source of his first play, writing the tragedy *Kullervo* in 1864 and initiating the medium of Finnish-language theatre. Finnish painters, particularly Akseli Gallen-Kallela (1865–1931) rushed to depict *Kalevala* subjects, enriching Finnish artistic life with images entirely divorced from the previous dominant cultures of Sweden and Russia – the tragedy of Aino, the vengeance of Kullervo, and the theft of the Sampo. Within only a few years, *Kalevala* subjects were highly visible, in frescoes, woodcuts and statues, injecting a powerful and unprecedented presence of Finnishness into the evolving critical conversation about art and life. Just as enduringly, the *Kalevala* also became something that could be *heard*, when the composer Johan 'Jean' Sibelius (1865–1957) began writing symphonies and tone poems on subjects including Kullervo and Lemminkäinen. The period of the *Kalevala*'s greatest flourishing as a theme, the 1890s, coincided with the rise of the arts and design movement known in Britain as Art Nouveau, and in Finland by its German title, *Jugendstil*. This, in turn, led to the peppering of central Helsinki with glorious cod-medieval follies – hotels, restaurants and offices built like castles and chased with carvings, frescoes and motifs drawn from Lönnrot's song-cycle, as if the buildings themselves are auditioning for a walk-on role in *Game of Thrones*.

Playing 'I-Spy' with *Kalevala* references can keep the visitor to modern Finland busy for days. It is not merely a case of street names and districts, statues and paintings, it leaps out at you in the supermarket and at the bank. Little rye biscuits are called Väinämöinen's Buttons. Pohjola, home of the money-making Sampo, is the name of a Finnish bank, as was Sampo itself until recently. Children from good Christian families are baptised with the names of pagan gods and heroes – it is entirely normal to run into a boy called Tapio after a Finnish forest god, or a girl called Aino, presumably named for the character's legendary beauty rather than her suicidal depression.

The *Kalevala* also influenced foreign writers. *Hiawatha* lifts much of the meter from its German edition, while the young JRR Tolkien was deeply moved not only by its stories, but by the idea that they had been reconstructed from the relics of a pre-Christian past. After attempts to write his own version of the myth of Kullervo, he would eventually embark on the creation of his own pseudo-mythology, positing an epic quest of demigods and heroes to forge and retain mythic magic jewels called *silmarils*. Tolkien created a language for his elves, Quenya, derived from Finnish itself. His love affair with the *Kalevala*, first mentioned in a letter to his fiancée as early as 1914, would eventually evolve into *The Lord of the Rings*.

However, not all is as it seems. Some might argue that the National Myth of the *Kalevala* is itself something of a myth. There was, and remains, some debate as to how much of the *Kalevala* is genuine forensic anthropology of ancient folktales, and how much of it was finessed and filtered by Lönnrot himself – Juha Pentikäinen's book *Kalevala Mythology* points to some persuasive parallels between certain events in Lönn-rot's own life and key moments in his song-cycle. Meanwhile, Derek Fewster, in his study of Finnish nationalism *Visions of Past Glory*, notes that while the *Kalevala* undoubtedly made an impression on certain sectors of the artistic community, the way its stories reached the general population was often second- or third-hand. The modern-day visitor to Finland is apt to believe that the *Kalevala* transformed the entire nation in an ecstasy of reading and response, whereas it had barely sold 130,000 copies by 1937. Instead, the most influential work in creating Finnishness was the *Book of Our Country*, published in Swedish in 1875 and Finnish a year later, by the author Zacharias Topelius. Topelius easily topped 340,000 sales in dual languages by 1908, becoming a school textbook, and hence the first point of contact that many Finns had with notions of Finnishness.

Intended for younger readers, Topelius toned down the sex and violence of other accounts of Finnishness. He was also apt to repeat ideas from some of his earlier works, when, as a younger man, he had written a somewhat Sweden-centric account of Finnish history. Like earlier Norse authors, Topelius was slippery in his use of the term 'Finn', sometimes referring to Saami, sometimes to Suomi, sometimes to scat-tered tribes that might one day make up Finnish ethnicity. 'Finnishness' was often parsed as an absence or an ignorance – the primitive, savage tribes of the Eastern Land, succumb-ing with great reluctance to the light of Swedish culture and Christian belief.

As a result, much of the 19th-century dialogue about the nature of Finnishness had to pull the concept up by its boot-straps, out of nothingness. Was there a Finnish 'kingdom' before the arrival of the Swedes? Since the Finnish lan-guage seemed to lack a native word for 'king', probably not. But what if the ancient legends of Finnish gods and heroes were actually garbled references to actual human beings? If the heroes of the *Kalevala* were once real people, and those people once led men and took wives, then surely that would point to an edifice of Finnishness?

What about religion? The Finns, according to all the Swedish records, were the savage barbarians who were forced at the point of a sword to convert to Christianity. So perhaps we might see Finnishness in Lalli, the murderer of St Henry? Maybe Finnishness can be reconstituted in opposition to St Henry's Catholic religion, by making a sign of true Finnishness to be the later, enthusiastic adoption of the more modern, Lutheran faith?

The academic and polemicist Johan Vilhelm Snellman (1806–1881) saw Finnishness as inherent in the language itself, and wrote articles, in Swedish, urging the upper classes of Finland to begin using the language of the Finnish majority in their daily life. Finnish grew in use in schools, and also in people's names, as Swedish speakers marked their allegiance to a sense of Finnishness by 'Fennicising' their names, often directly translating the meaning of their Swedish surname into its Finnish equivalent. Aleksis Kivi, the author, had previously been Alexis Stenvall. Aleksi Gallen-Kallela had begun his life as the plainer Axel Gallén. Kaarlo Ståhlberg, later Finland's first president, had been Carl Ståhlberg before the movement, and so on.

The search for Finnishness became of greater importance towards the end of the 19th century, when Russia's benign policies towards the Grand Duchy became increasingly proscriptive, and the Finns began to push back.

4

A Nation is Born: 1899–1939

FINLAND IS FESTOONED with statues of Carl Gustaf
Mannerheim. Today his effigy walks with a jaunty step in
the central town square of Mikkeli, where his statue was con-
troversially moved after spending the Cold War somewhere
less visible; as it were, only having his victory parade when
the coast was clear. He walks his horse unheedingly past the
Finnish parliament building on the Helsinki street that bears
his name; a rival equestrian design trots insolently outside
Lahti train station. He lurks a little hesitantly in a Seinäjoki
park, and there's even a bust of him right here in my Jyväskylä
office. But Tampere's Mannerheim statue is very different,
tucked away in a forest on a hilltop on the outskirts of the
town. A notice beneath the statue reads that it was 'from this
hill' that Mannerheim looked down at the Battle of Tampere
in 1918. It neglects to add that the statue was originally commissioned to stand in the centre of Tampere, but that events
conspired against it.

The original idea came on the 20th anniversary of the
Battle of Tampere, when the rich local industrialist and
former council leader Rafael Haarla proposed a monument
to the leader of the 'Whites'. It was already a provocative
move – as a member of the ruling class and a supporter of
the anti-Communist Whites, Haarla had been stabbed and
assaulted in 1918, and was determined to ram home the

message that his side had prevailed. He died in 1938, but the project to build the statue went ahead, despite the objections of Mannerheim himself, who really didn't like the idea of being commemorated before he was dead.

The Second World War led to the postponement of the plans, and by the time the dust had settled, Tampere's council had swung far to the left. Mannerheim was, by that time, a different kind of national hero (see Chapter 5), but the Tampere statue was blatantly provocative, aping the clothes and pose of a famous portrait of White Mannerheim from 1918, not the defiant Marshal of Finland of 1939. Horrified that they had inherited a giant bronze image of the man who had rounded up Finland's Reds, the socialist council prevaricated for a while, and then decided on a compromise, siting the statue of their nemesis out in the sticks. Perhaps, in itself, this was a commentary on Mannerheim's role in the Battle of Tampere, subtly suggesting that he should have come a bit closer to the town in order to see what was being done there in his name.

The original intended base of the Mannerheim Statue now hosts a memorial to the White soldiers. The original intended site is occupied by a shepherd-boy nude, flanked by a couple of sheep, commemorating the 150th anniversary of a local cotton mill. Mannerheim, meanwhile, stares down at the city he once attacked. In 2004, he was voted the Greatest Finn of all time in a national TV survey. The next day, someone daubed a single word in red paint across the base of his statue: *Lahtari* (Butcher).

Russification

The Russian honeymoon began to fade by the 1880s. The growing power of Bismarck's Germany, and the growing unrest within the Tsar's Empire itself, placed the ruler under stronger pressure to bring Finland more firmly into the fold. There were already signs in the 1880s that the growing

Finnish nationalist movement faced stronger opposition in the government of its Grand Prince, but the real effects did not begin to show until the death of Alexander III in 1894.

He was succeeded by his son Nicholas II, remembered today as the last of the Romanovs, but better known in Finland as 'The Perjurer' for what is perceived to be his betrayal of the Tsar's traditional oath to uphold Finnish autonomy. In 1899, Nicholas produced the stern, unequivocal February Manifesto, announcing that from now on, only roubles would be legal tender in Finland. The Finnish post office would now use Russian stamps, and the official religion of state was now the Orthodox Church.

Nicholas followed this in 1900 with a Language Manifesto that decreed Russian to be the official language of administration. A year later, he signed a Conscription Law that effectively abolished the Finnish army, obliging Finns instead to join up in the Russian military, where of course, the language of administration was also Russian. With only 8,000 Russians in the Grand Duchy, 2.5 million Finns were effectively relegated to second-class citizens, unless they could very swiftly learn the language of their masters.

In Finland, these reforms were regarded as a coup d'état, wiping out decades of promises and goodwill made to the supposedly autonomous Finns by successive Tsars. Nor was it possible to protest quite so freely as before, since the press was now subject to a Russian censor.

'We have found it necessary to reserve to Ourselves the final decision,' wrote Nicholas, 'as to which laws come within the scope of general imperial legislation.' Or in other words, every single scrap of freedom permitted to the Finns since 1809 was merely at the sufferance of the Tsar; freedoms were only leased, not permanently granted.

In 1898, Nicholas had appointed a new figure to implement these measures, his hatchet-man Governor-General Nikolai Bobrikov, an aging military officer who looked like Ming the Merciless with *pince-nez* spectacles. Bobrikov is remembered by the Finns as an awful despot, although Russian accounts present him as a driven, loyal man, determined to do the right thing by his Tsar, working all hours and weakened by a series of heart attacks. He arrived in Finland to conduct a brief inspection tour, and came away distinctly unimpressed.

'Everything proved that Finland has nothing in common with the Empire,' Bobrikov observed. 'I felt as if I were travelling in a foreign country. And this is the closest borderland to the Empire's capital, a region which is strategically very important.'

Bobrikov tightened the Tsar's hold even further, decreeing that the number of school lessons taught in Russian should be increased, and demanding that all correspondence between institutions also be in Russian.

The Finns fought back in a number of protests. A petition circulated, but met with no worthwhile response. The artist Akseli Gallen-Kallela designed a black 'stamp of mourning' bearing a golden Finnish lion, which Finns duly glued to all their envelopes as a quiet protest about the Russian stamps. Meanwhile, when the day came for the new Finnish conscripts to enrol for their Russian army duty, more than half failed to show up. Bobrikov was granted dictatorial powers, but Finns were not pressed to join up, as the Tsar's army no longer trusted them anyway. This sudden frosty attitude towards the Finns caused new troubles for the Russians, when someone in the maritime office realised that almost all the pilots on the ships that arrived in St Petersburg were from the now allegedly disloyal Grand Duchy. One carefully timed strike among the pilots, and St Petersburg could be shut down from the sea. Hastily, the Russians convened a new pilot school to rush through some presumably more loyal men.

In 1904, Tsar Nicholas II went to war at the far eastern end of his new Trans-Siberian Railway, fighting a disastrous conflict against Japan. The Russo-Japanese War of 1904–1905 has sometimes been called World War Zero for its use as a testing ground for many of the innovations of the later conflict – including the early designs for dreadnoughts, barbed wire, trench warfare, wireless telegraphy and sea mines. But even as the Russian war machine was grinding into action, Finland risked becoming a fifth column of unrest on the Tsar's doorstep. Several anarchist groups hatched plans to assassinate Bobrikov, although all were beaten to it by a man supposedly acting alone. Eugen Schauman, a senator's son and former clerk who knew his way around the Senate building, sneaked in through a back door in June 1904 and accosted Bobrikov on the stairs.

Schauman had been practising with his Browning pistol for weeks, and was a sure shot. He fired off three swift rounds, all of which hit the Governor-General. Then he turned his pistol on himself and shot himself twice in the heart, dead before he hit the ground. Bobrikov's many medals deflected two of the bullets, but the third shattered on his belt buckle and wrecked his stomach. He did not die until the following day, after a tense vigil in which the Russians were never quite sure what the Finnish crowd outside the hospital was praying for.

Condemned as a terrorist, Eugen Schauman was buried in an unmarked grave, although he was later moved to his family tomb (see Gazetteer: Porvoo). The site of the assassination is marked by a discreet plaque in the hallway of what is now the Finnish prime minister's office, reading in Latin: *Pro Patria Se Dedit* (For his country himself he gave). As with Lalli of legend (see Chapter 1), Finland defined itself through brutal opposition to foreign influences.

There was some controversy over whether or not Schauman was really acting alone. Certainly, the Russians were very suspicious that a prominent Swedish newspaper should not only report on the incident the following day, but seemingly have a photograph of the assassin ready to run, as if parties in Stockholm already knew it was going to happen. It was also not lost on the Tsar's enemies that the Finns were ready for direct action, leading the Japanese secret service to plot a daring act of espionage, designed to distract the Tsar from the Far East by creating trouble on his doorstep.

The Japanese military attaché in Stockholm, Moto-jiro Akashi, was given a million yen in cash, and told to do everything he could to stir up the Finns. Akashi, a lone man 'worth ten divisions' in the eyes of the Japanese high command, hatched a plan to undermine Russia by starting a revolution in its most volatile territory. He assembled an unlikely multinational group of agents, led by Konni Zillia-cus, a committed revolutionary who acquired an aging tramp steamer, the *John Grafton*, bought in the name of a Stepney wine merchant and stocked with thousands of rifles, pistols and rounds of ammunition, all bought by agents claiming to represent the King of Siam.

Owing to a misunderstanding with the aforementioned wine merchant, the *John Grafton* was also loaded with several hundred gallons of wine, which the Finnish crew had already begun to work through by the time the ship was in the North Sea. Zilliacus, meanwhile, unwisely chose this highly stress-ful secret mission, with his crew unconvincingly disguised as members of the Southampton Yacht Club, to try to give up smoking – leading to an embarrassing set-to with the police in Copenhagen where he was caught trying to break into a tobacconist.

After several more misadventures in the Baltic, the *John Grafton* eventually reached the Finnish coast, which it located by unceremoniously ramming into it. Trapped in the shallows of Ostrobothnia, the crew began unloading their cargo, only to be surprised by a vessel from the Russian navy. Realising that time was tight, they ran up the red flag, saluted it, and then ran for dear life while a lit fuse sparked the onboard explosives.

The explosion of the *John Grafton* was heard two counties away. The Tsar's men inspected its twisted wreckage (see Gaz-etteer: Pietarsaari), and fearfully reported on the conditions of the many hundreds of rifles that had been landed before the explosion. Although the revolutionary mission had been a failure, the mere fact of the existence of the *John Grafton*, and the possibility that it was only one of many ships, was a source of great concern to the Russian state. However, it had taken care of most of Akashi's money, and he would soon be run out of Europe after some of his meddling correspondence was made public; he ended up as governor of Taiwan. Konni Zilliacus, meanwhile, fled to England, and would write his memoirs and a cookbook. In one of those odd footnotes of history, his namesake son became the Labour MP for Manchester Gorton.

Revolution: Whites vs Reds

Despite such dangers in Finnish waters, with Russia's defeat and destabilisation in the war with Japan, Finland still seemed like a safer place for the Tsar himself than his own empire. Tsar Nicholas II came nowhere near Finland for the first decade of his reign, but became a regular sight there in the 1900s, after his security detail informed him that they could no longer guarantee his safety in Russia proper. Seemingly not seeing this for the awful portent that it was, Nicholas took to cruising the Gulf of Finland on his beloved yacht *Standart*.

'For the tsar, it is the only way to spend a real holiday,' wrote Baroness Sophie Buxhoeveden in her memoirs. 'While in Finland, he gave up formalities of the court and lived a more simple life. He got daily reports from his ministers in the capital, but they would take up only a part of his day. The greatest part he spent as he pleased, hunting, canoeing or playing tennis, all of which are pleasing pastimes for the emperor.'

Finland was a pleasanter realm for Nicholas II partly because the defeat in 1905 had led to a general relaxation of his earlier Russification policies. With the Tsar conceding a 'Duma' (parliament) in St Petersburg after post-war protests, the Finns also gained a greater degree of political freedom, with the first decade of the 20th century seeing the formation of several parties whose influence continues today – both the National Coalition and the Social Democrats, two of the major parties in modern Finland, began in slightly different forms in the brief thaw post-1905. By 1907, however, the Tsar was flexing his muscles again, and the Finns found themselves pressured to 'Russify' once more.

In 1914, Germany declared war on Russia, plunging the Tsar and his dominions into a conflict in Europe, and causing mass lay-offs in the Finnish timber industry, which lost many of its European clients. Otherwise, however, the early days of the First World War caused something of an economic boom in Finland, with massive increases in demand for Finnish paper, dairy products and food to supply the Russian army.

In 1917, Russia's fading fortunes in the war, and unemployment in its cities combined to form the events of the 'March Revolution'. Finland responded in July 1917 by proclaiming itself independent from Russian rule, a bold and somewhat foolhardy move for a state without its own army. Instead, the peacekeeping lay in the hands of two rival local militia, the right-wing Whites and the left-wing Reds.

The division of Finland into Whites and Reds is arguably the greatest of its national tragedies, all the more so because many of them shared similar aims. Most wanted an independent Finland – ironically the pro-Tsarist Whites in Russia refused to consider an independent Finland, whereas the Bolshevik Reds under Lenin paid lip-service to the idea of one, which they hoped would rejoin Russia as a Soviet republic. With the collapse of Russia's political government in the second (i.e. 'October') Revolution of 1917, Finland became a site of simmering tensions, infested with nests of Russian soldiers with uncertain allegiances, and roving bands of militia.

The south of the country, its urban centres including Turku, Viipuri and Helsinki, was claimed for the Reds, although a number of White politicians smuggled themselves out of the capital and formed a rump government on the coast (see Gazetteer: Vaasa), ahead of the Red Terror that saw over 1,600 White sympathisers murdered. Vaasa hence became the centre of the White counter-attack. Local White militia neutralised Red enclaves and Russian outposts with whatever weapons came to hand, including the notorious confiscated Grafton rifles, mothballed in storage for over a decade, and now finally put to a revolutionary use.

The leader of the White military forces was Carl Gustaf Mannerheim (1867–1951), a baron of the Finnish nobility who had served 30 years in the Russian army. Mannerheim had enjoyed a relatively undistinguished career, specialising in two areas of expertise that were overtaken by technology and politics. He had previously been a cavalry specialist in the era that saw the introduction of the internal combustion engine. He had then specialised in Far Eastern matters, in the expectation that Russia would one day fight a rematch against Japan in Chinese territory – a war long on the cards, but forever postponed by the Revolution. By 1917, he was a lieutenant general, the highest-ranking Finn in Russian service, and despondent at the treatment his country had received. Fleeing revolutionary Russian by the skin of his teeth, he arrived back in Finland to find himself appointed as the leader of the White forces, in command of an army of well-intentioned farmers, aging former officers of the disbanded Finnish army (idle for a decade), or soldiers, like him, whose service to the Tsar made others suspicious of their motives.

Mannerheim led the White forces from their Vaasa redoubt in a campaign that would swiftly seize the important hubs of the railway network, pushing back against the Red forces and driving them ever further to the south and east.

His most controversial victory was at the Battle of Tampere in 1918, a hard-fought conflict over the city that straddled the railway connection to Helsinki. Tampere proved to be the decisive battle of what had become the Finnish Civil War

– its fall would leave the Reds in the south open to attacks from either flank.

But Tampere was controversial because of the high loss of life. A series of men lost to Red snipers led to the indiscriminate use of grenades against any movement in buildings – sometimes with tragic results. A thousand Whites perished in the fight over the city, and double the number of Reds. But some ten thousand Reds were taken prisoner, many of whom died in custody of maltreatment, starvation or disease. However, Mannerheim had accorded his opponents the military distinction of regarding them as enemy combatants – by his decree all surrendered Reds should be treated as prisoners of war, and accorded due process. But the flipside of Mannerheim's distinction, not immediately recognised by many of his supporters, was that Reds who broke the terms of their surrender would also be treated with military procedure. The implications of this only became clear in the aftermath of the White victory, when any attempts by Reds in occupied territory to stir up unrest, such as blowing up a bridge or assaulting a soldier, would be met with summary execution for acts of military espionage.

The Civil War would end with a mass exodus of the Reds into Russia, where many fared badly at the hands of the new Soviet state – leading to a deadpan Finnish joke that Stalin was a great man because he had killed a lot of Communists. If the story of Finland's Reds seems under-represented in today's public life, it is because many of those that weren't killed in the conflict faded into the landscape of Soviet Karelia, emigrated to North America or Australia, or disappeared in one of Stalin's many purges. Although the split into Red and White is a common subject in many Finnish films and novels, few of these have been translated. The national memory of the Revolution and/or Civil War is one of the White victory, and the sense that Finland, of all the Tsar's domains, was the only one to stay clear of Communism after the October Revolution.

Mannerheim's own sister, who had worked as a nurse in Red Helsinki, had written to him pleading for merciful treatment for prisoners, arguing that the Reds she had met were largely good-hearted people with a sense of loyalty to an independent Finland. But her words were largely lost in a bitter conflict that set neighbour against neighbour, split families forever, and saw the settling of many petty scores under the guise of patriotism. The story of the civil war is rich with tales of petty fights and intimidations – the White soldiers in Lahti who stole the Reds' artillery when they left it outside a pub; the Red sympathisers in Jyväskylä who nailed shut all the doors of pro-White shopkeepers; the two Red prisoners in Viipuri shot for merely *suggesting* that they might be rescued by a counter-attack from over the border; the many lynchings and assaults conducted against men in Red areas seen as 'landlords', or women in White areas seen as 'Russian brides' (female Red supporters in trousers were often assumed to be combatants and treated as such; those in skirts merely as collaborators).

The resentment of the Civil War would simmer among the Finns until the Second World War presented them with a greater enemy against whom they could unite. But even today, it occasionally bubbles to the service, in small, angry acts such as the vandalism of Mannerheim's Tampere statue.

The Jaegers and 'King Väinö I'

There is another side to the Finnish Civil War, of huge importance at the time although it, too, has largely been swamped by later historical events, and that is the involvement of the Germans.

Mannerheim only accepted the position as leader of the White forces on the understanding that he would be leading Finnish soldiers. Ever the strategist, he was worried about the implications of winning the battle for Finland with foreign aid – there were already Swedish peace-keepers landed on the

Åland Islands, whom he suspected of plotting to wrest the territory away from Finland. He was thus immensely angry and, eventually, grudgingly grateful for the arrival of troops from yet another foreign power, the Kaiser's Germany.

During the period of attempted Russification, many patriotic Finns, particularly from wealthier families with foreign connections, sneaked out of the country or were exiled for anti-Russian sentiment, and made their way through Sweden to Germany, where they enlisted in the German army. The 27th Prussian Jaeger Battalion, which fought for Germany in 1916, contained some 1,100 Finns. Eventually some 2,000 strong, they returned to Finland in the middle of the Civil War, bringing much-needed skills and experience to the White side.

The Jaegers arrived as an incredible morale boost to the Finns, although much to their annoyance, many of them were dragged out of their units to train less able men who lacked their experience. Just to whip up everybody's martial ire, the composer Sibelius cranked out a stirring hymn, the 'Jaeger March', to lyrics written by Jaeger Heikki Nurmio:

Deep is our blow, our wrath invincible,
we have no mercy, no homeland.
Our fortune rests on the tip of our swords,
our hearts cannot fail.
Our war cry rings, enchanting the nation
that is severing its chains.

And so on, only slightly ruined for modern ears by the chance echoes in its opening bars of the theme from *The Muppet Show*.

The Jaegers, however, also brought some friends with them – 10,000 German soldiers of the Baltic Sea Division under the command of Rüdiger von der Goltz, whose arrival constituted a second front against the Reds. Mannerheim, who had spent the early part of the First World War fighting against the Germans as a Russian officer, was deeply mistrustful of the Kaiser's motives, rightly suspecting that Germany was hoping to secure influence over a new Finnish satellite state to keep it supplied with raw materials. He did, however, have to concede that the Germans were vital in securing several southern sites, including Turku and Helsinki itself, where the arrival of German allies may have even saved Finnish lives by preventing a retaliatory bloodbath of Reds by victorious Whites.

Although the Jaegers are famous in Finnish history, and would form not only the core of the new army of independent Finland, but a powerful faction within the early Finnish government and institutions, the Baltic Sea Division is less well known. The Germans did not march in Mannerheim's victory parade in Helsinki, allowing Mannerheim and the media coverage of the day to remember it as an entirely 'Finnish' achievement. According to von der Goltz's memoirs, published in 1920, this was his own idea in order to preserve the Finnish sense of achievement; he crept away with his men to fight on in Latvia, leaving the Finns to establish their newly-won state.

Von der Goltz remained respectful and enamoured of Finland, commenting in his memoirs that Finland was the only place where Germans were still welcome 'with open arms'.

> Germany won a *new friend*, the only friend to remain true to it, who did not turn away ... with revulsion and disdain ... We Germans will not forget that about Finland. All of us, though, who were allowed to contribute to this ... are proud to have taken part in the sole surviving success from this world war.

It was not the last time that Finns found themselves almost entirely alone, only to be rescued by German allies. This was certainly a contributing factor in the next request for aid from Germany, when a monarchist faction within the new

Finnish government asked if the Germans could lend them a king.

The previous monarch of Finland, at least technically, had been Tsar Nicholas II, already dead by Bolshevik firing squad in Ekaterinburg. There were already factions within the government calling for a presidential republic, but monarchists, favouring a Swedish-style king, enjoyed a marginal majority at the critical time of May 1918. So it was that a Finnish envoy was sent scurrying to Kaiser Wilhelm II, with a request that his fifth son accept a notional crown of Finland, and become its first king.

The son in question was unavailable, as was Duke Adolf Friedrich of Mecklenburg-Schwerin, who had been proposed as the grand ruler of a unified Baltic Duchy, incorporating not only Finland, but also Estonia and Latvia.

By September 1918, the Finnish Diet had its man, Prince Friedrich Karl of Hesse, the Kaiser's 50-year-old brother-in-law. Rüdiger von der Goltz approved, noting that the prince and his wife were famously down-to-earth, and that it was this 'great straightforwardness and naturalness that recommended him to the democratically-minded Finns.'

Although the parliament was still locked in debate, with the appointment of 'King Väinö' still not quite gaining the two-third majority required by protocol, the prince was confident enough to begin Finnish lessons with his wife. He embarked at a leisurely 90 minutes a day, which, in the author's own experience, would have allowed him to order a beer in a restaurant after only another year of study. Truth be told, most Finns were less enthused about the aging Friedrich than they were about his dashing young son Wolfgang, already being billed as Finland's crown prince, and lined up for a meeting with eligible young Finnish debutantes in the search for a local bride.

But 1918 was precisely the wrong time to get into bed with Germany. Finnish hopes of securing German political support were fast dwindling, as was Germany's ability to keep its own house in order. It was Mannerheim who sternly warned the monarchists that Finland could not afford to be seen to ally itself with the defeated Kaiser's Germany, but as late as October 1918, there were still elements within the Finnish government trying to entice Prince Friedrich over.

In the end, it was Friedrich himself who called a close to the idea, asking for two months to consider the offer. By the time his self-imposed deadline had passed, Germany had been defeated, the Kaiser had abdicated, and the Finnish senate had instead approached one of their own, offering Mannerheim the role of Regent of Finland. Mannerheim returned from meetings in London with the news that the British would recognise the newly-formed state of Finland on several conditions, including the cancellation of any invitation to any German monarch.

Friedrich ended the charade on 14th December 1918, officially rejecting the crown, and leaving Finland no other realistic option but that of a republic. Regent Mannerheim arrived back in his homeland two days later, and served in that role for six months, until elections returned the lawyer KJ Ståhlberg as Finland's first president.

The Kingdom of Finland was nothing but a fantasy. Its crown, designed but never made, was eventually created in replica in the 1980s by curious Finnish artisans. Its putative king died in 1940, as the Head of the House of Hesse. Two weeks after his funeral, an envoy arrived from the Finnish embassy in Berlin, and discreetly laid a wreath on his tomb.

Crown Prince Wolfgang died in 1989, the last surviving great-grandchild of Queen Victoria.

Racing the Storm

The debate on what 'Finnishness' should be only intensified after the foundation of an independent state. Many of those who fought to establish it found themselves marginalised and unwelcome in the new nation, including Mannerheim himself, who stood unsuccessfully for president and then slunk away into quiet semi-retirement, muttering dire portents about the need for more military funding and the threat of a Russian attack.

Communism had been declared illegal in 1918, but that didn't stop various front organisations and left-wing parties gaining large shares of the vote – the remaining Red sympathisers remained a voting bloc with some strength, threatening to turn Finland into a Soviet state by force of democratic will. Women, meanwhile, who had had the vote in Finland since 1906, were a major influence on the ratification of a 1919 Prohibition law, which turned Finland into a supposedly alcohol-free state (complete with 'fortified' teas and speakeasies) for the next 13 years (see Eating and Drinking: Alcohol).

American food aid helped stave off starvation in the war-wrecked country, leading to the 1920s Finnish slang term for sponging: 'living off [President] Hoover'. Finland turned its attention largely to Europe, conducting barely 1% of its trade with the Soviet Russian state on its border. As Josef Stalin rose to power in the Soviet Union, Russian rhetoric about Finland became increasingly agitated, painting it as a far-right dictatorship, run by a junta of Red-hating rebels. By the 1930s, Stalin was secure enough in the Soviet Union to begin talking of regaining 'lost' territories from the Tsar's era.

Mannerheim referred in his memoirs to a sense of 'racing the storm' in the 1930s, as the League of Nations struggled to keep reins on disputes. One of the international body's only successes was its ruling that the Åland Islands, disputed between Sweden and Finland, should be Finnish territory, winning Mannerheim a diplomatic victory and keeping the islands in Finnish hands to this day (see Gazetteer: Ahvenanmaa). But elsewhere the League was increasingly powerless, leaving the Finns largely on their own as Stalin's negotiators arrived to demand concessions in the south-east. When Finland had been a Grand Duchy, the fact that its borders were so close to St Petersburg was not an issue. Now it was independent and anti-Red, it represented a dangerous threat practically on the city limits of what was now the city of Leningrad.

Russian behaviour became increasingly bullish, and the situation increasingly tense, while Mannerheim, now back in the administration, demanded better funding for Finland's military to deal with a rising threat. Eventually, he resigned in frustration. Barely two days later, on 26th November 1939, Russian artillerymen on the border shelled one of their own positions, creating an immediate crisis, accusations of a Finnish attack, and a Soviet 'counter'-offensive. The Winter War had begun.

5

In the Cold: 1939–1991

Some of the winter war trenches on the Raate Road are still maintained, kept clear of debris and vegetation, walled in with planks and wooden pilings. You can wander among the snaking front lines, crouched half-hunkered against imaginary shrapnel, and stare through the peaceful forests at the places where once the Russians were.

There are howitzers and armoured vehicles scattered outside the Raate Road Museum, and the baked ruin of a Russian tank, twisted and fired in some terrible conflagration. Inside the museum proper, the battle over the Raate Road is picked out in a vast diorama with toy vehicles and little painted figures and railway-model fir trees. It shows the moment that the elite Soviet 44th division mistakenly decided to enter Finland uninvited, via the Raate Road. On 5th January 1940, amid temperatures that fell below 40 degrees Celsius, the Russians, unused to skis and not all that keen on snow, were ambushed by 300 Finns.

Even the model itself is scary. The gunmetal-grey Russian column of tanks and troop transports is scattered across 30 feet of model forest, strewn with model horses laying on their side, and toy soldiers trampled in the Hornby train-set snow. White-clad Finns, ghosts in the snow with pistols, knives and axes are dotted through the model forest. It looks as if several toy buses have hit several herds of toy reindeer, the Manson family let loose on a Nativity scene. Roughly halfway down the column, there is figure in a white dress, face down in the snow with a pistol in her hand.

Outside the museum, in a vast area of cleared forest, there is a figure-of-eight pathway with a shamanistic-seeming structure at its centre. Seen from a distance, the Winter War Monument looks like four sets of giant antlers leaning on each other. Its graceful curves support a latticework of bells – 105 little chimes ringing in the wind, one for each day of the hostilities.

It sits in the middle of a blasted field with jagged rocks, numbering some 20,000 – one for every life lost on both sides. It is, supposedly, 'polynational', designed in 2003 by Erkki Pullinen to meet the needs of several museums and organisations on both sides of the border, to commemorate the lives of both sides. But the Finns around the monument tell a different story. One pats one of the large boulders reverently, explaining: 'These are the Finns.'

He leans down and scoops up a handful of gravel.

'This,' he whispers, 'is the Russians.'

There are also separate monuments on the road itself.

The one for the Finns is fraught with all the pretensions of modern art. It is a big ... thing ... by the roadside. Some say it is Stalin's accusing finger. Others that it is a howitzer at rest. Nobody seems to know. Somewhere, an artist found a bit of metal, welded it to a plinth, and sold it to the Finnish government.

The Russians have their own monument, too, by the road in the middle of the woods. It is a weeping woman, sunk to her knees in anguish, clutching at a cruciform staff for support. Past the statue is an area of boggy ground, crossed by walking on duckboards across the sodden earth. Somewhere beneath your feet are the unrecovered bodies of 79 Russians, who never made it out of the marsh.

The Winter War

Despite only occupying six years of Finland's history, the Second World War was definitive in establishing the Finnish sense of nationhood and state of mind. Its repercussions echo today, in Finland's continued absence from NATO, in Finnish men's continued obligation to perform national military service, in candle-lit autumn graveyards and stoically observed flag days.

For the Finns who lived through it, it was greeted as the end of the Red-White rivalry, with Mannerheim (dragged out of retirement again) calling on the people to put aside their old enmities to fight a greater foe. It briefly cherished a dream of a Greater Finland stretching all the way to the White Sea, before rudely awakening the Finns with the loss of 10% of their territory. The Maid of Finland suffered the loss of one arm (the Petsamo region, reassigned from Russia in the 1860s, now snatched back for its nickel mine) and some serious liposuction around her hips (most of Karelia) – some 410,000 Karelian Finns fled west to be settled in post-war Finland.

The war also solidified the Finns' reputation for bloody-minded tenacity: they were admired in the international press for their stoic resistance against overwhelming odds; then pitied for their abandonment to the whims of realpolitik with the Russian switch in sides; then reviled for signing their controversial co-belligerency pact with the Nazis. The Finnish term *sisu*, for sheer guts, briefly entered the international lexicon; indeed, many Finns are still surprised when visiting foreigners have never heard of it.

The Russians had begun by demanding territory from the Finns for strategic purposes – the Hanko peninsula, former sight of Princess Alvild's legendary Viking raids, as a port for the modern navy, and territory in the south-west to roll back the border from Leningrad. When these 'negotiations' bore little fruit – the Finns being unwilling to simply hand over territory because Stalin wanted it – his foreign minister

Vyacheslav Molotov ominous declared that it was 'time for the soldiers' to do the talking.

Sixty-five men, women and children died in the first bombing raids on Helsinki, while Molotov snidely commented that the Soviet aircraft were only dropping 'food parcels' for the local population. In later battles in the east, Finnish soldiers would return the culinary insult by hurling 'Molotov cocktails' at the Russians – the first use of what is now an international slang term for a petrol bomb.

Meanwhile, in the eastern Finnish town of Terijoki (see The Lost Lands: Zelenogorsk), the Finnish Communist Otto Kuusinen suddenly declared the foundation of the Finnish Democratic Republic. Terijoki had only recently been evacuated by the Finns, which makes one wonder where Kuusinen got his population from, but the move was plainly calculated to reignite the Red/White stand-off, offering Finnish Reds an apparent alternative to the incumbent government. Kuusinen's puppet state, however, was overwhelmed by current events – the prolonged Finnish resistance to Russia would prove to be so powerful that even Stalin would eventually negotiate with the real government, cancelling any potential value of the Red splinter state. Today, Terijoki (or rather Zelenogorsk) is still a station on the train line from Helsinki to St Petersburg, but the mainline trains don't even slow down for it. Blink and you'll miss it, a bit like the Finnish Democratic Republic. Kuusinen's proclamation was also very obviously an act of Russian propaganda, to the extent that it actually disgusted many of Finland's honest-hearted Reds, and led them to proclaim their allegiance to Mannerheim. One story of the Winter War recalls a former Red serving in the Finnish army, blithely observing that he was rather pleased that the 'Butcher in Chief' who annihilated them at Tampere was now in charge of defending the whole country.

Mannerheim ran his defence out of a train command centre and a scattered series of buildings in Mikkeli (see

Gazetteer: Mikkeli). The real action, however, was down on the Karelian Isthmus where Finland met the outlying regions of Leningrad Oblast, and where a 'Mannerheim Line' of fortifications significantly slowed the Soviet advance.

The Soviet numbers were overwhelming but the soldiers were poorly trained and badly supplied. Many of them had yet to work out that it was inadvisable to throw a grenade ahead of oneself when skiing; many lacked adequate winter clothing; few had any experience of winter fighting. The Finns literally ran rings around them, luring them onto lake ice and dynamiting it under their tanks; attacking tactical bottlenecks of moving columns, leaving thousands of troops stuck behind damaged vehicles; ambushing them from the trees.

The Finnish reputation for *sisu* gained some of its most notorious examples. Regardless of the size of an attacking air squadron, the Finns would always send at least one plane up against them, hoping for a lucky shot against overconfident bombers. There are stories from the Winter War of Finns with pistols single-handedly trying to take out tanks by aiming through the tiny eye slits; of attacks targeting not the Soviets' heavy gear, but their morale-maintaining soup kitchens; and of night attacks where Finns fell upon Russians huddled two-to-a sleeping bag in cold conditions, and slitting just one throat per pair, leaving the other to wake up next to a cold and bloody corpse.

Low-tech was the order of the day. Finland's most famous sniper, Simo Häyhä, notched up 505 kills in the Winter War, using a basic rifle without a scope. He claimed it allowed him to keep his head a fraction lower, and avoided the glint of the scope's glass potentially alerting his targets. Such behaviours all served to fatally bog down the Soviet advance. The Soviet plan on the Raate road in the north was to cut Finland in half at Oulu. Instead, despite outnumbering the Finns five to one, the attempted *blitzkrieg* rush to the coast advanced with agonising slowness. Often, when the Russians did advance, it was only because the Finns had hatched another devious ambush a mile ahead.

Not even Mannerheim believed the figures. He once sent a brusque communiqué to one of his front line commanders, demanding fair and accurate assessments of military actions, and not wild claims such as that of killing a thousand Russians in a single night. The officer at Taipale responded with characteristic Finnish bluntness, telling his commander-in-chief that he had a pile of a thousand Russian rifles, and Mannerheim was welcome to come down and count them himself.

Winston Churchill flagged the success of Finland in its fight against Communism in his 'House of Many Mansions' speech, 20th January, 1940.

> Only Finland – superb, nay, sublime in the jaws of peril – Finland shows what free men can do. The service rendered by Finland to mankind is magnificent ... Many illusions about Soviet Russia have been dispelled in these few fierce weeks of fighting in the Arctic Circle. Everyone can see how Communism rots the soul of a nation; how it makes it abject and hungry in peace, and proves it base and abominable in war ... If the light of freedom which still burns so brightly in the frozen North should be finally quenched, it might well herald a return to the Dark Ages, when every vestige of human progress during two thousand years would be engulfed.

However, Finland fought on alone. In March 1940, the combatants came back to the table to negotiate, resulting in the Peace of Moscow that ceded parts of eastern Finland to the Soviets. The desperate Finnish holding action had served its purpose, keeping the country from falling to the Soviet Union at a terrible cost. The treaty specified that the roads, bridges and towns of Karelia should be left intact, but when the Russians moved in, they discovered they had forgotten to stipulate that the Finns should remain. They marched into ghost towns, devoid of people, and often with the cultural treasures stripped away (see Gazetteer: Joensuu). In churches all over Finland, a signed decree from Mannerheim can usually still be found framed on the wall, awarding a medal to the 'mothers of Finland' for their own sacrifices.

The Continuation & Lapland Wars

The end of the Winter War came as something of a surprise for the Finns in Helsinki, who had heard nothing but stirring tales of derring-do, and had started to assume that the strong resistance could go on indefinitely. Mannerheim had a far better idea of the exhaustion of his men and resources, and knew that the time was right to call it before his hard-won line began to buckle. Having served in the Russian military for 30 years, Mannerheim was well aware of his former masters' policy of seizing as much territory as possible, with no intention of holding it, and then ransoming it back to the enemy for gains elsewhere.

The peace lasted for two whole months before the Russians began pushing for more concessions. Mannerheim had warned all along that this would happen, and had spent many weeks pleading with the government that the war was not over, merely on hiatus.

In 1940, the poet and professor Veikko Koskenniemi wrote lyrics to 'Finlandia', a musical piece by Sibelius that dated back to 1900 and the height of the Tsar's Russification programme. It remains one of the songs that is most likely to rouse the passions of the Finns, possibly even more than their national anthem (see Publishers and Authors) – its opening, at first sight at least, seems rooted in the struggle for Finland's independence in the 19th century, only for allusions to gather of the conflict that was still raw in Finns' hearts.

O, Finland, behold, your day is dawning,
The threat of night has been banished away,
And the lark of morning in the brightness sings,
As though the very firmament would ring.
The powers of the night are vanquished by the morning
    light,
Your day is dawning, O land of birth.

O, rise, Finland, raise up high
Your head, wreathed with great memories.
O, rise, Finland, you showed to the world
That you drove away the slavery,
And that you did not bend under oppression,
Your day has come, O land of birth.

I have cornered Finns at parties and restaurants, and asked
them open-endedly to tell me what this song means to them,
curious as to whether they associate it with the 1900 of the
tune or the 1940 of the lyrics. Universally, Finns have recalled
sights of snow and combat. Universally, they have begun
humming the tune and mouthing the lyrics. Universally,
their voices have cracked on the penultimate line *'ja ettet
taipunut Sa sorron alle'* (And that you did not bend under
oppression).

It became something of an anthem of the Finns' sudden
counterstrike against the Russians, which began in June 1941.
It is remembered in Finland as *Jatkosota* (the Continuation
War), in Russia as The Great Patriotic War, and in Germany
as Operation Barbarossa. In a controversial move, Finland
signed a 'co-belligerency pact' with Hitler's Germany, resup-
plying its own forces with crucial German materials, but also
allowing German troops to transit Finland in secret, ready to
fall upon the Soviet border in a surprise attack.

Mannerheim remained wary of the Germans, as he had
been in 1918, and was keen to stress that he had not formed
an alliance with the Germans, merely agreed that since

both had a common enemy, they would fight alongside one another. This distinction was lost on many Finns, particularly in the north of the country, where the German divisions were welcomed as inheritors of the old Jaeger goodwill of the Civil War days, and received with such open arms that Finns were heard to grimly jape: 'The Russians took our men, and the Germans took our women.'

In imitation of the Jaegers of old, a number of Finnish men had also volunteered to serve in the German army, forming a component of the 5th SS Panzer Division. Largely comprised of foreigners from the Baltic region, from which it drew its historically minded nickname 'Wiking', the 5th SS Panzer Division fought on the Eastern front, at Stalingrad and in the Caucasus, at Kharkov and Kursk, before the increasingly defensive actions saw them moved back into Poland and Czechoslovakia. By then, however, the several hundred Finnish volunteers had long been withdrawn and sent back to Finland to bolster the troops in the Continuation War – they had been ordered home at Mannerheim's request, and he forbade any further enlistment of Finns in German battalions.

The Continuation War was an unprecedented success. Finns, aided by strong German advances at their flanks, swiftly snatched back the lands that had been lost in the Winter War, and kept on going. With Helsinki presses and publishers, newly pro-German, fulminating about the need for *Finnlands lebensraum* in the East, Mannerheim's men took back East Karelia all the way to the shores of Lake Ladoga, but stopped, tantalisingly short of Leningrad. There was substantial argument in Finland about the wisdom of this action – regaining stolen ground was one thing, but actively invading and appropriating Russian territory was not necessarily what many Finns had signed up for. Such issues also characterised the affable, ever-polite but increasingly apprehensive communiqués between Mannerheim and Churchill, as the British Prime Minister gingerly warned the

Finnish Marshal that if matters continued in this way, Britain would be forced to declare war on Finland, despite their long friendship.

'I wish I could convince Your Excellency that we are going to beat the Nazis,' wrote Churchill, 'It would be most painful to the many friends of your country in England if Finland found herself in the dock with the guilty and defeated Nazis.'

Britain did eventually declare war on Finland, at least on paper. But it was perhaps with Churchill's warning in mind that the Finns executed the next and final turnabout of their Second World War. As a Soviet counter-offensive pushed the Finns out of Karelia and drove them back to their 1940 borders, the Finns turned on their German allies, ordering them out of the country, and then attacking any who were slow to get the message.

This 'Lapland War', named for the northern Finnish realm where most of the Germans were stationed, led to the destruction of most buildings north of the Arctic Circle (see Gazetteer: Rovaniemi), as both the Finns and Germans demolished any sites that might be used by their enemies. The Germans were certainly taken aback by the sudden reversal – one can still sometimes spot the faded traces of graffiti in the area reading: '*Danke für nichts*'. They left behind wives, girlfriends and children, although many hundreds of Finnish women chose to leave with their German husbands, the subject of Virpi Suutari's 2010 documentary *Auf Wiedersehen Finnland*.

But the Lapland War, while a cruel and devious reversal, would serve Finland well after VE Day. Although some Finnish politicians would be locked away for their dealings with the Nazis, Finland itself avoided occupation or invasion. Although the Second World War would cost Finland some 10% of its territory, it remained free, albeit in hock to the Soviet Union for war reparations – despite the many thousands of miles of borders shared by the Soviet Union with other countries, only Finland and Norway among them were democracies with market economies. Appointed by the Finnish parliament as an interim ruler, Carl Gustaf Mannerheim ended his active career as President Mannerheim, serving until March 1946, when the transfer to peacetime was considered done.

Finlandisation

For the much of the rest of the 20th century, Finland walked a tense, jumpy line, carefully preserving a neutral status while sharing a thousand-kilometre eastern border with its greatest historical enemy.

Finland's seventh president, Juho Paasikivi, had formerly been the ambassador to Moscow, and steered the country through treacherous waters. Finland may have preserved its independence in the Second World War, but remained perilously close to the Soviet Union and Soviet influence. 'Wisdom,' said Paasikivi with a shrug, 'begins with acknowledgement of the facts.' And the fact was that should conflict ever break out again, Finland would once again be likely to face the Soviet Union alone.

The Paasikivi Doctrine was one of 'active neutrality', with Finland doing its level best to not make any sudden moves that might annoy the Russians. This was continued by his successor Urho Kekkonen, in office from 1956 to 1982, under whom Finland exercised careful censorship of inflammatory or anti-Soviet media, and maintained a cool disinterest in NATO, in order to avoid being press-ganged into the Warsaw Pact.

Some undiplomatic diplomats, carping from the safety of the free world, began to refer to 'Finlandisation', with the implication that Finland had been somehow infiltrated and tainted by the Soviet Union. During the long reign of President Kekkonen, the term 'Kekkoslovakia' was also used as a pejorative by the Finns themselves, suggesting that Finland was practically in the Soviet Union's pocket. But Finland's delicate position cut both ways. Finnish politicians were just as fearful of NATO, since if war broke out and the Western powers mounted an attack on Russia through Finnish airspace, the Finns would be unable to stop them, and would then face the risk of a Russian counter-strike similarly crossing Finnish territory.

Kekkonen is not a well-known figure internationally today, although his domination of Finnish politics for four decades (he was prime minister before he was president) has left him so recognisable to the Finns that the simple depiction of his iconic 1950s spectacles is enough to recall his era – his visage still decorates the first pub you reach after disembarking in Tallinn from the Helsinki ferry, designed to lure Finns in for a patriotic drink before they have barely taken a step on Estonian soil.

In 1961, he summarised his political position to the United Nations by saying that the Finns wanted to be 'physicians rather than judges' in superpower politics. 'It is not for us to pass judgement nor to condemn, it is rather to diagnose and to try to cure.' To some extent, he was even successful – Finland's war reparations to the Soviet Union, intended to cripple it post-war, were not only paid in full, but in such a manner as to turn Finland into one of the Soviet Union's major trading partners. As conditions thawed, Finland was reframed not as a former enemy suffering financial punishment, but as an example of the kind of peaceful trade relations it was possible for the Soviet Union to have with the outside world.

Contemporary Finns are insulted by the notion that their country is in 'Eastern Europe'. They try at all times to push the notion that they are one of the 'Nordic Countries', practically Scandinavian in their outlook and background. But the mid- to late-20th century saw Finland pursue its careful neutrality in the grim shadow of Moscow, with restrictions on criticising the Soviet Union only finally relaxing in the late 1980s, as the rise of Mikhail Gorbachev heralded the downfall of Communism. Ironically, this would also cause a deep recession in Finland, when many of the country's east-facing trade contacts collapsed. However, by the 1990s, with the Soviet Union's power dwindling, Finland could finally come in from the cold.

Lapponia

Meanwhile, with wartime associations inadvisable, the sense of Finnishness retreated once more into myth, albeit myth that was carefully sanitised for an international audience. Throughout the years, Finland's Eurovision Song Contest entries represented the usual carnival of nutters, offering ill-considered ditties about nuclear war, meaningless lyrics about waterfowl, and even an awful attempt at reggae. In the midst of all of it in 1977, Monica Aspelund delivered a beautiful, moving song about doomed love beneath the Aurora Borealis – 'Lapponia', translated into six languages, charting high in several countries' hit parades, and usually entirely mistranslated as some sort of tourist brochure. This is the dreadful English version:

> If you need to get away
> I know someplace where we can stay
> Far away from the city, it's peaceful every day
> Why don't we get on a plane tonight
> And head for the Northern Lights
> Where you can be happy
> So sing along with me now.

Despite being initially commissioned as an advertising jingle to sell Lapponia-brand sheds, the original Finnish lyrics are very different: a fantastic and chilling evocation of ancient Lapland, laden with menace and wonder. Here it is translated from the original Finnish:

That girl is a witch
Who conjures with destinies
Without company or solace
And so she weaves her magic
Creating with the power of spells
So with sorcery she may summon a man.

Said man duly arrives, a 'human man of Earth' in the lyrics of the original song, who falls in love with her, only for her to fly away, *Käy tulella taivaan ja loitsut kaikuen soi* (She goes with the fire of the sky and the spells echo). Aspelund's lyrics are rich with the cadences of the *Kalevala* and the archaisms of Saami sorcery, but go and listen on YouTube: it will sound nothing like what you first imagine.

It's difficult to think of something quite so heavy-metal as this topic, but Aspelund's lyrics were shoe-horned into a piano melody by Aarno Raninen – it would be 33 years before the rock band Northern Kings gave it the properly bombastic version it really warranted. But the fate of 'Lapponia' only goes to show the immense pressures on Finnish creatives to somehow cram their rich poetic traditions into the demands, or supposed demands, of the international mainstream. In a country with less than 5.5 million people, it perhaps only makes sound business sense to sing in English and tick the right boxes for MTV. Finns speak perfect English by necessity, and have little trouble integrating themselves into the Americanised hit parade in the forms popularised by bands such as Hanoi Rocks, HIM and the 69 Eyes. But a few strike out, like the folk group Värttinä, determined to hang onto their Finnishness in subjects and language, drawing their lyrics from ancient spells and love ballads. Finnish artists, in many media, often face a brutal choice between remaining forever a big fish in a small pond, never filling a venue bigger than a town hall, or removing so much of their Finnishness to sing in English and appeal to the Americanised MTV world that they hardly seem to be Finns at all.

6

Finland in the 21st Century

LINNUNLAULU ('BIRDSONG') now largely comprises parkland around Töölö bay, an inlet of the Baltic that sits like a lake in the middle of Helsinki. A pathway snakes around the water's edge, hosting joggers, dog-walkers and strollers. Just off the track, there is a 2.7-metre imposing stone slab, bearing a familiar symbol of three triangles within a circle, and a list of dozens of names.

It looks like any other war memorial that one might expect to see in a European park, although this is nothing to do with any war. It is the *Itsekkyyden Muistomerkki* (the Memorial to Selfishness), erected by Greenpeace in 2010, bearing the names, districts and party affiliations of 129 Finnish politicians who voted in favour of nuclear power.

It is an oddly mobile monument. Before it was fully carved, it sat outside the Finnish parliament building like a gravestone, bearing the ominous PR-nightmare legend on a sash: 'Do you want your name here?'

Since its completion, it has wandered the city like Banquo's stony ghost, popping up in slabby scorn outside the railway station, before finally coming to semi-permanent rest next to Töölö bay. One imagines certain politicians having recurring nightmares, that they might wake up to find it at the foot of their bed like the head of some Mafioso's prized racehorse. The Memorial to Selfishness is a fantastic icon of modern Finland. Its initiator, the marketing manager Veera Juvonen, has a masterful grasp of propaganda, and a suitably Finnish bluntness when it came to naming and shaming the politicians. The permanent, enduring implications of nuclear power are carved in suitably long-lived stone, granite that will last for millennia, like the nuclear waste itself, long after the transient day-at-the-office that the voting surely comprised for many of its participants.

The Monument to Selfishness is the result of the growing controversy over the Olkiluoto power plant. Defenders of Olkiluoto counter that it is an order of magnitude safer than Chernobyl, and has an environmental footprint substantially smaller than that of, say, the 120,000 windmills that would be required to replace it with green energy. It was also intended as the main pillar in fulfilling Finland's emission-reduction obligations under the Kyoto Accords – sometimes, one gets the impression, as ever, that the Finns are one of the only nations actually taking it seriously. In a quintessentially Finnish battle of wits and politesse, protestors outside the facility were beckoned in for a tour, to see its technology for themselves, but refused, perhaps understanding how accepting such an invitation might play into the hands of their rivals' public relations.

Some Finnish wags have even suggested that Olkiluoto itself serves as a monument to the spirit of the 21st century, not in terms of the hope of cleaner, safer nuclear power, but as a preposterous boondoggle that has run so far over budget that it is now 'too big to fail'. The construction of its third reactor, originally scheduled for completion in 2010, and now at least eight years late, has been dogged by safety considerations and code violations, as the strict parameters of nuclear power plant construction fox the skills of a largely immigrant workforce. Having promised to absorb any cost-overruns, the original construction company has now backed out, leaving the project still unfinished. With projected final costs now standing at €8.5 billion, the lead companies on the project are busy in a finger-pointing battle over who should take responsibility for the many delays, while the media archly reports that Olkiluoto is now one of the most expensive structures in the world, with an estimated cost now greater than that of Europe's Large Hadron Collider. Meanwhile, digging continues at nearby Onkalo for the construction of a nuclear waste disposal vault suitable to keep radioactive materials undisturbed. Finns are still arguing over the best way to post danger signs that will still be legible in 100,000 years' time. After discussions over monoliths and symbols, or a 'landscape of thorns' made from giant concrete spikes, the general consensus seems to be that the best policy is to hope that future civilisations simply forget it is there at all.

With the third reactor incomplete, and unlikely to be finished any time before 2020, the Finnish parliament voted for construction to begin on yet more generators, with more modest aims. It was this decision that led to the commissioning of the Monument to Selfishness, encapsulating not only the mistrust of many voters in the long-term safety of nuclear power, but in their elected representatives' apparent willingness to throw good money after bad.

Nokia & Linux

Although energy issues hound the politicians all over the world, Olkiluoto and Onkalo have some uniquely Finnish qualities. One gets the sense with Olkiluoto that many of its problems have been caused *because* of the Finns' traditional diligence in following rules and regulations. And Onkalo's impressive temple of radioactivity is only possible in Finland, where the rocks have already had several billion years untroubled by quakes and tectonic movements, and it seems to be worth risking storing nuclear waste within them for a few paltry thousands. At least Finland *has* a scheme for permanent disposal of nuclear waste.

However, technology in general has been kinder to Finland since the 1990s, when the chance confluence of several forces and innovations made Finland a prime mover in the global digital economy. The Nokia Corporation began in the industrial revolutionary era of the 19th century that saw lumber mills and cotton mills springing up near the rapids of Tampere. It had slowly accreted from a rubber company, a wood company, and several other ventures, moving almost by accident into telegraphy and electricity generation in the 20th century. By the 1980s, a lucrative contract with the Finnish armed forces had caused the company to experiment with wireless telephony, and the canny purchase of its leading competitor left it a market leader in the growing sector of what were first called 'car phones,' and then, as they became smaller and more efficient, 'mobile phones'.

By 1987, Nokia had established a global standard in 'second generation' phones, which is to say, ones that could not only call other phones, but also send text messages. Within a decade, Nokia had become the world's largest manufacturer of mobile phones, and would remain so for 13 prosperous years, until everybody and his dog had a cellphone, and competition from Android and iPhone operating systems crushed the company's lead.

For many foreigners born at the close of the 20th century, Finland is a word associated not with any historical narrative, but with modern developments in digital technology – not just the big-bang pandemic of mobile communications in the space of a single generation, but the rise of applications and open-source software. Linus Torvalds, a student at Helsinki University, released an operating system in 1991, which he would literally give away to the online community. Linux, as it came to be known, is now the basis of millions of computers and systems, and only the most fundamental and widespread of many Finnish initiatives in open-source software and content.

And then there are the ones you pay for, like *Angry Birds*, released in 2009 by Rovio Entertainment, a company which took its name from its hometown, Rovaniemi. Although it makes up to 45% of its revenue from merchandising and spin-offs, *Angry Birds* remains one of the most successful mobile phone applications ever created, marking the move of much of the Finnish telecoms industry out of hardware and into software. Even Nokia has gone down this route, with its primary business bought by Microsoft – it no longer makes the phones, but continues to work on the programs that run on them.

Satan & Santa

Finland in the 21st century enjoys an international footprint far outweighing its meagre 5.5-million population. Its most conspicuous and, frankly, unexpected achievement came in 2006, when after decades of novelty acts, petrified jailbait and weary lounge singers, Finland's entry to the Eurovision Song Contest swept the boards with a landslide victory.

From the moment it won the pre-selection Song for Finland, 'Hard Rock Hallelujah' was clearly something of a lark. The rock-band Lordi, attired in horror masks, with bat-wings and a battle-axe that shot fire, belted out heavy-metal bombast a world away from the *kum-ba-yah* internationalism of most Eurovision winners:

> The saints are crippled
> On this sinners' night
> Lost are the lambs with no guiding light
> The walls come down like thunder
> The rock's about to roll
> It's the arockalypse
> Now bare your soul

Fortunately, most of the Catholic countries couldn't hear the lyrics properly. Even more luckily, Eurovision's recently inaugurated continent-wide tele-voting began around the time that half the Western world's pubs were evicting their giggling students and embittered Goths, ensuring a 'protest vote' that propelled Lordi to unprecedented heights.

The morning after the night before, the Finns suddenly found themselves not only part of the international community, but sitting at its very centre, having inadvertently won a contest with more viewers than the Oscars. In London, the Finnish ambassador was hauled over the coals by the BBC, asked if he felt his country's culture was best represented by horned demons singing about Armageddon, and was clearly too shocked to make the logical riposte that the British entry that year had featured a creepy rapper in a yellow leather jacket, standing in a classroom full of off-key schoolgirls.

The likelihood that many of Lordi's votes were bestowed ironically was lost on many Finns, who swiftly collapsed into exuberant triumphalism. For a nation that barely seemed to care what Eurovision was before May 2006, there was suddenly dancing in the duck ponds and excitable rooftop yells of '*Arockalypse!*' The country went Lordi crazy, with the introduction of Lordi pizzas, Lordi calendars, Lordi masks, a Lordi comic and a Lordi restaurant. Although much of the euphoria has now faded, the band's presence can still be felt in their hometown, where their demonic handprints adorn the local square (see Gazetteer: Rovaniemi). Musically, rock remains the drug of choice among many young Finns; the bored visitor can easily entertain themselves by timing how long it takes for Bryan Adams or Bon Jovi to turn up on the radio, and there is something rather sweet about the laundry section in Finnish supermarkets, which offers washing powder for whites, colours and *blacks*.

At the time of Lordi's success, Finland's other popular international claim to fame was in financial difficulty. Santa Park in Rovaniemi had been founded in 1998 by a UK-based corporation, funded by an intricate web of Finnish interests, including the airline Finnair, the Finnish post office, and a Finnish TV channel. For a country only recently integrated into the European Union, the prospect of a Santa-themed theme park was a wonderful piece of synergy, drawing on off-hand references in folklore to Father Christmas living in 'Lapland', and deviously rushing to put such a park in the Finnish part of Lapland, rather than say, Norway's.

Rovaniemi was an ideal location, sufficiently far from Helsinki to be reachable by a romantic overnight sleeper train, but also with air connections to the rest of Europe. Seasonal charter flights could transport large quantities of foreign tourists for a Christmas experience complete with real snow, real reindeer, and a convincingly avuncular Santa Claus. It was also far enough north to offer a reasonable chance of seeing the Aurora Borealis, and conveniently close to the physical line of the Arctic Circle – always a good photo opportunity. In 2009, the majority ownership of the park was transferred to two local Finns, who continue to push it as a global Christmas destination, including sleigh rides, a trip to Santa's workshop, and the ominous-sounding elf show.

My Homeland is Finland

Finland aspires to be a classless society. All men are equal when they are sitting in the sauna – a truism taken to literal conclusions in the Finnish army, where salutes are not required in addressing fellow nudists. Finns have little time for bespoke tailoring – regardless of one's profession, the unity of air-conditioned environments behind the triple-glazed windows, and the ubiquity of the snowstorms outside, soon favours a population in ski-wear in the street, and shirt-sleeves in the office. When summer rolls around, the Finns strip off with barely-concealed glee, embracing the brief warmth in a flurry of lakeside barbecues and skinny-dipping.

Sometimes, to the outside observer, they seem to take even the fun a little seriously. Ask a company director what he is doing at the weekend, and more often than not he will wax lyrical about his simple log cabin and the pleasures of chopping wood by a smoky fire. Particularly in the north, outside the metropolitan areas of the south, most Finns are only a couple of generations removed from farmers and foresters. Government healthy-eating initiatives have gently pressured them to take more salad and eat less lard, the calorific demands of pushing around a computer mouse somewhat dwarfed by the previous dietary requirements of woodsmen and milkmaids. Modern Finns remain wary of obesity and alcoholism, both easy temptations in an era of American super-sized portions and all-you-can-eat buffets (see Chapter 7: Eating and Drinking).

Finland's education system is the envy of the world, prompting frenzied conferences as far away as Shanghai attempting to work out the secret of Finnish kids' success at school, despite spending the least amount of combined time on classes and homework of any industrialised country. Speaking from first-hand experience, a lot of the success of the Finnish education system is down to the simple fact that it is chock full of Finns, gently cherished by a social security system that ensures square meals for all and a good home environment. The Finnish education system is also, to all intents and purposes, *free of charge*. Given a choice between idling one's way through a master's degree or entering the workplace to pay tax, many Finns simply take the student option, packing Finnish industry with graduates.

The tension in Finland comes in the second generation, where parents recently arrived in the middle class often have trouble persuading their offspring to put in the school hours required to stay there. Finland is not crime free – certain suburbs, in particular, have statistically unremarkable incidents of robbery, burglary and drugs – but the problem that vexes many police to a greater extent is juvenile delinquency, not of hopeless thugs from broken homes, but of over-entitled rich kids who have grown up thinking that everything should be handed to them on a plate, and troubled by the realisation that work is still required.

Finnish education also happily calves off the more practically-minded into vocational training in their teens, creating a ready army of cooks, beauticians, hair-dressers, plumbers, carpenters and electricians. In one of many beautifully simple and palpably beneficial incentives in Finnish law, all households are eligible for an annual tax break for home improvement and domestic services, as long as the money is spent on accredited labourers. This generates massive demand for painters, decorators, builders, child-minders and cleaners, finding ample employment for many vocational school graduates, but also ensuring that their work is run through the system and taxed. Not only is Finland mercifully short on cowboy builders, but most homes are suitably ready to brave the next harsh winter.

Finland spent much of the late 20th century attempting to worm its way into the international community. It joined the European Union and embraced the euro with great alacrity. It lucked into the worldwide exponential growth of mobile telephony, and scored several software hits, including the ongoing spread of Linux, and the unstoppable fad of *Angry Birds*. Affluent Finnish yuppies are the quintessential snowbirds, thronging to the Canary Islands, Crete and Thailand in the winter months, to clog beaches, bars and diving schools. But internationalism does not seem to be quite as welcome at home. Finland takes its quota of refugees, but immigrants have a tough time fitting in with such a complex and peculiar language, and into a population that is already naturally wary of outsiders.

The canny foreign observer can racially profile the genetic background of the average Finnish crowd with some degree of success, into elfin, flaxen-haired Swedes, impish, dark-haired Finns, almond-eyed, high-cheekboned Saami, and the occasional pointy-nosed Russian. But Finnishness, that national trait so nobly fought for, was defined for decades as a genetic and ethnic phenomenon. To *be* Finnish, one had to be from Finland; one had to have great-aunts from Karelia and a shed in the forest, an ancestor who once worked on the tar boats and a grandfather with a funny story about the Winter War. Finnishness ever since the semi-legendary Lalli has been about standing one's ground against new-fangled foreign ideas and arrivals – an idea that has returned to bite the nation's think-tanks in the cosmopolitan 21st century, when European citizens like the author can up stakes and move to Finland with only the merest scribble of paperwork, when tourists from (*whisper it ...*) *Russia* can make or break the takings of a summer spa resort, or when the best chance of securing jobs at the local mill is attracting the interests of Chinese venture capitalists.

The average Somali or Thai has substantially greater difficulty integrating into such a privileged sense of Finnishness, particularly when faced by the usual right-wing spite common to urban areas, and an epicurean deficiency peculiar to Finland, that is strongly resistant to any 'foreign' food that is not pizza or a kebab (see Chapter 7: Eating and Drinking). Nor might one really expect them to – for every gruff and unemployable Finn on the dole, snarling into his beer that some immigrant has taken his notional job, there is a Somali in a puffa-jacket and a bobble hat, skulking with his friends outside the railway station and bemoaning the pointlessness of having to learn Finnish when his ultimate aim is to drive a taxi in South London.

In the TV series *Mogadishu Avenue* (2006), the writer Jari Tervo made a bold and uplifting statement of unity by simply having the multi-ethnic cast sing the theme song – a rainbow coalition of races all belting out 'Kotimaani Ompi Suomi' (My Homeland is Finland). His point, common to multiculturalists the world over, was that these people were born in Finland, went to Finnish schools, grew up speaking Finnish, and now were merrily paying Finnish tax. Was that somehow not enough? But many Finns remain in a self-fulfilling cycle of intercultural ignorance and benign racism, unaware, for example that the common term *neekeri* is best (and then barely acceptably) translated as Negro rather than nigger.

But in the ferment of Finnish political parties, the anti-immigration, anti-Europe Finns Party (*Perussuomalaiset*, formerly translated as True Finns, more literally, the Basic Finns) has made exponential gains, becoming the largest opposition party in 2011 with 19.1% of the vote.

The question of Finnishness in a wired world found its ultimate artistic expression in a truly bonkers enterprise, seen by both right and left wings as a triumphal illustration of their concerns, when the national television broadcaster YLE funded Gilbert Lukalian's production of *The Marshal of Finland* (2012), a film about Mannerheim, made in Kenya with an all-black cast. Presumably, for some earnest commissioner in an air-conditioned Helsinki meeting room, this was a good idea, stretching precious euros by filming in a cheap location, generating massive publicity for a televisual event, and demonstrating to the world that the story of Mannerheim was so internationally alluring as to attract the interest of African film-makers.

The Finns went into uproar. A poll in the tabloid newspaper *Iltalehti* unconvincingly argued that 90% of Finns would refuse to tune in. The right went into conniptions about the sight of the hallowed Mannerheim being played by a black actor, while even the liberals were heard wondering if the whole thing wasn't an elaborate double bluff – a facetious, knowing carnivalisation of Mannerheim's reputation by depicting him in a Z-grade movie. People wondered, and are still wondering, to what extent the Kenyans were piously telling a story (leading man Telley Savalas Otieno certainly seemed serious about his role), or cynically milking gormless media lefties for boondoggle funding.

It all went to show, in a world where you can buy a Mannerheim cookbook, a Mannerheim comic, and a Mannerheim puppet show, that the word Mannerheim is almost as sure-fire a money-spinner with Finns as the word Moomin.

YLE certainly generated vast publicity and newspaper column inches, getting not only their movie but also a six-part documentary about the making of the movie. And of course, they had generated 'debate', in much the same way that children taunt each other with imaginary blinking powder. But their decision was also divisive and underhand, taunting the audience with a provocative gesture, and daring them to raise objections and sound like racists.

There will be more statues. There will be more songs. Finland in the 21st century approaches its centenary in 2017 as a vibrant parliamentary democracy, a modern republic and a state deeply enmeshed in the new Europe. The question of what constitutes 'Finnishness' remains as debatable as always, ever since that legendary medieval day on a frozen lake, when a man struck a bishop with an axe and began the story of Finland.

7

Eating and Drinking

FINNISH FOOD achieved international notoriety in 2005, when the gaffe-prone Italian Prime Minister Silvio Berlusconi proclaimed that it was awful, and the Finns a bunch of philistines who 'don't even know what parma ham is.' With matching charm, France's Jacques Chirac later agreed, observing sagely that it was even worse than *English* food – itself a running joke in Europe ever since Olaf the Stout chuckled at King Canute stuck in Cabbage-land.

The Finnish food industry fought back with what, for Finns, was a stinging rebuke, although Berlusconi might well have countered that they had made his point for him. A red onion, mushroom and smoked reindeer pizza, known as 'the Berlusconi', went on to win the 2008 New York Pizza Show, beating Italy into second place.

Notably, many international restaurant critics also sprung to Finland's defence, citing superb, world-class meals eaten in Finnish restaurants. Since 2011, Finland has also been the epicentre of the International Restaurant Day (*Ravintolapäivä*) – pre-agreed dates, now several times a year, when pop-up eateries spring to life on street corners and verandas. However, while it is true that good food does exist in Finland, we might timidly concede that Berlusconi could have been onto something.

As long as you are prepared to pay, not only is good food within your immediate grasp, almost anywhere in Finland outside the smallest village, but also the Finn who sells it to you will know appreciably more about its preparation and suitability than you do. The grade inflation caused by Finland's free education system has put immensely knowledgeable people into every sector of the food industry, from farmers to waiters, and it is entirely normal for your butcher to have a master's degree in meat technology, and for your grocer to be a postgraduate agronomist.

In the Finns' defence, the immense freshness of their locally-sourced food, and the prospect offered by the natural winter temperature for refrigeration, may have combined to create a palate that avoids the spices and condiments of warmer countries. But Finnish cuisine has always had the odds stacked against it, with a short growing season, thin soil and limited resources, so that even cattle need special protection. The Viking sagas marked one particularly harsh winter by wailing: 'Like the Finns have we our bud-eaters bound in barns.'

In part, the Russian era is also to blame, particularly for a culinary tradition that offered a table of free nibbles, while only expecting the patrons to pay for the vodka. A French chef in St Petersburg once gave Gustaf Mannerheim a tongue-lashing for knocking back tastebud-numbing schnapps at the beginning of a meal.

But one also gets the sense among many Finns that food is little more than fuel to them, best cheaply sourced and swiftly tanked. Perhaps as a relic of their hard-working, farming past and the likelihood of inclement, freezing weather outside, Finns are far more likely to have a hearty breakfast and all-but ignore lunch, further reducing the opportunities for dining as a public, social occasion. Faced with a nice French meal for double the London price, or a crispbread and something from the salad bar, the average no-nonsense Finn is liable to go for the latter. Monty Python's hymn to 'a snack lunch in the hall' was presciently accurate, since there seems to be little acceptance of the more Mediterranean custom of time taken with multiple courses and conversation – Finns not being famed for the latter. There is also an invisible undercurrent influencing Finnish dining, which is that the rival money-off programmes of the S-cards and the Plussa cards have effectively sewn up much of the Finnish high street and shopping centre. These loyalty schemes offer all sorts of perks, from free parking to free toilet access in affiliated stores, as well as discounted eating, all of which steers the average Finn in search of lunch towards a mega-mall full of chain restaurants, to the detriment of any finer or more localised dining.

The worst enemies of Finnish cuisine are the Finns themselves, an overwhelming majority of whom seem happy with all-you-can-eat buffets and tasteless dole. Meanwhile, the free healthcare system's willingness to categorize almost anything as a 'condition' has fostered a culture of needlessly fussy eaters. Many are the world-class, Michelin-worthy Finnish chefs and restaurateurs I have observed, biting their lips and trying not to go crazy with a meat cleaver, as local diners ask them if it's possible to have the onion soup without any onions in it. A Thai restaurant in Jyväskylä, now sadly defunct, once placed a sign on every table that spoke of the cooks' recurring anguish with their unappreciative clientele. It read as follows:

We cook our food to Finnish standards.
If you want it done properly, let us know.

Try to interest a group of Finns in fine dining and listen in torment as one claims not to like 'foreign' food, and another regards anything above eight euros as too much to pay for lunch. Inevitably, they will then start comparing their alleged allergies and intolerances, and before you know it, you, too, will be muddling through at a pizza buffet in customary silence. But at least you've got some more points on your Plussa card, so you can save money on Persil.

All of which amounts to a simple warning – there is great food to be had in Finland, but it is not cheap.

Food

'The flavour of our cheeses has been much praised,' claimed Daniel Juslenius in 1700, although the author has found no evidence to back this up. Finnish cuisine favours forest products and game – mushroom soups and reindeer stew. Avoid the cans of 'bear meat' on sale at the airport – they do contain traces of ursine DNA, but have been bulked up with so much cheaper meat that a more honest butcher might label them as a different animal altogether.

'We have one special dish which is not found elsewhere,' writes Juslenius with evident pride. 'It is made by boiling rye malt and, after placing it in a birch basket, baking it like bread in an oven. This food is dark but extremely sweet. It is called *mämmi*, and it is eaten on Easter Day in memory of unleavened bread.' Finns often seem to regard eating *mämmi* as some sort of test of endurance for tourists; accept the challenge, since it tastes like nothing so unusual as liquidised malt loaf.

Finns also seem oddly proud of the *kalakukko*, a fish baked inside a loaf of bread, and the Karelian pie (*Karjalan piirakka*), an open-topped rye pasty. The worst of them taste like cardboard; the best taste of nothing, but are supposed to be rendered edible with a generous spread of eggy butter (*munavoi*), usually to be found close at hand. These are relatively common in hotel buffets, and may form your first encounter with genuinely Finnish food.

Otherwise, Finnish chefs often try a little bit too hard to incorporate that nebulous sense of 'Finnishness' into other dishes, and default to garnishing everything with berries. The lingonberry, huckleberry and cloud berry are particular favourites, but the Finns have almost as many berries in their repertoire as allergies, and are sure to sneak a few into your food if you are not looking.

The Swedish era left its mark with several regional cuisines and customs, particularly the orgy of crustacean abuse that arrives each year with the crayfish season. Finnish salmon, i.e. *gravlax*, is excellent, as are any other lake- or Baltic-sourced marine dishes you are liable to encounter. As in Sweden, pea soup (*hernekeitto*) is served on Thursdays, with a dash of mustard to give it some zing. This tradition continues in the military, where the ease of preparing it in bulk is appreciated, and often crosses over into public life for the same reason, with pea soup forming a staple part of Finnish school dinners, and even handed out by the mugful by tub-thumping politicians cultivating an image of homespun approachability. If my late father-in-law had his way, my own wedding would have ended with a barrel of pea soup in the forest, thereby making it possible to invite everybody in Central Finland.

The forensically-minded can have a lot of fun trying to work out which foreign food is being approximated with Finnish ingredients. 'Swedish' meatballs, for example, seem to be distant facsimiles of the Greek *kieftedes*, picked up on the edges of the Ottoman Empire by King Karl XII during his Moldavian exile. There is also a *Finnish* meatball – the sauce is different – although the only place I have ever seen Finns eat them is in the dining car on the train to St Petersburg, where they defiantly order them the moment the train is over the border. Similarly, Greek *dolmades* (stuffed vine leaves) seem to have been very roughly jury-rigged in Finland as cabbage rolls (*kaalikääryle*), although almost all the original ingredients have been supplanted with something not-quite-sufficient, and insult is usually added to injury, as usual, by someone throwing in a handful of berries to ruin the flavour. Meanwhile, many are the Germans who have scoffed in disbelief at Finnish sausages, pointing out that they are indeed very rough facsimiles of actual sausages. Although quality bangers can be had from any supermarket, starting at a steep €1 each, the average Finnish sausage is a dismal, charmless tube, seemingly created in the glum expectation that it is liable to be burnt on a forest barbecue anyway.

Russia's influence has largely waned on main courses, although Finnish supermarkets still do a brisk trade in Smetana sour cream and *pasha*, a delightfully rich Easter custard – the Russian name was originally *paskha*, but unfortunately that is a homonym in Finnish for excrement. One other odd legacy of the Tsar's Empire is *vorschmack*, a salty meat dish of mashed herrings, onions and offal, served with pickles and sour cream, and supposedly a delicacy brought back to Finland by Gustaf Mannerheim after his service as a regimental commander in Poland. This tall tale is so well established that the leading brand is Marskin Vorschmack ('the Marshal's Vorschmack'), but beyond that, you are on your own. It looks so repulsive that I have not been able to bring myself to ever try it.

Spend any time dining with Finns, and you may notice that much of their apparent disinterest in food evaporates when dessert comes around. The average Finn, it seems, will happily gargle sawdust and gnaw on iron filings as long as there is ice cream for afters. Finnish ice cream, eaten all year round, even in winter, is an unexpectedly classy affair, coming in many excellent flavours, including the rare variants of liquorice, *terva* (wood tar), and the salty *salmiakki* (ammonium chloride). The Finns are also hugely proud of their cakes, buns and tarts, none of which seem remotely remarkable.

During the Cold War, it was often said that the world's best Russian food could be found in Helsinki, and the capital remains an epicurean delight. Particularly in the centre, it offers fine selections of international cuisine, as well as high-class dining in the European style. Outside the capital, however, fine dining opportunities swiftly decline, and the visitor to most other Finnish cities is liable to exhaust the opportunities to try new restaurants in the average weekend.

Finland did not get its first pizzeria until 1969, although the modern visitor would be forgiven for thinking it was the national dish. Local additions like reindeer and chanterelle mushrooms add a dash of variety to Finnish pizzas, and you can be sure to find someone ready to rustle up a Berlusconi. Much fast food outside the usual chains and the local Hesburger cafés seems to be in the hands of hard-working Turks and Eastern European immigrants, who are doing their level best to establish the kebab as a staple food.

One chain worthy of note is Harald, a 'Viking' restaurant that deftly avoids reminding diners that Vikings didn't actually come from Finland, although they might have occasionally robbed it. There are currently eight branches across the country from Helsinki to Oulu. Although the cuisine is mainly modern, it tends towards ingredients that would have been available in the Middle Ages, and has a mead-hall ambience that is sure to include your steak being delivered on the point of a sword, a cheese board served on a piece of longship oar, and fellow diners donning historically inaccurate but always entertaining horned helmets. It'll look better on Instagram than yet another picture of you shovelling a cheesecake into your face.

Drink

It's when the Finns drink that their non-European origins become most obvious, not the least at the average Finnish breakfast table, where one brand of milk is never enough. The baffled visitor will often encounter pasteurised milk, skimmed milk, semi-skimmed milk, fat-free milk, cream, *coffee* cream, sour milk, fortified milk, and usually also a lactose-free, fat-free *milk*-free milk so removed from everyday cow juice that European Union food regulations insisted its name be changed to Milk Drink (*maitojuoma*). And that's before you get to the yoghurts. One senses here the distant undercurrent of Finland's past, when a nation of dairy farmers tried boldly to pretend they weren't all carrying lactose-intolerant Asian genes, or perhaps an indicator of Finns' habitual hypochondria, where everybody needs to feel special, even when putting something on their cornflakes. Marry a Finn, and doom yourself to endless arguments about precisely *what kind of milk* someone meant by putting the lone word on the shopping list.

In the world of soft drinks, Finland has the usual roster of fizzy fruit flavours, plus a few that supposedly taste of berries. The most distinct local drink is arguably *sima*, a very low-alcohol mead, usually drunk in the spring.

Alcohol

And then there is that other gene, the one that has trouble breaking down alcohol. Finns have always been legendary drinkers, such that Elias Lönnrot, on his posting to Kajaani, was dumbfounded at what passed for abstinence – only consuming hard liquor with meals, and once every couple of hours.

Said Voltaire of the Finns in 1731:

> The climate is severe; there is scarcely any spring or autumn, but there are nine months of winter in the year ... The people ... live to a good old age when they do not undermine their constitutions by the abuse of strong drink, which northern nations seem to crave all the more because they have been denied them by Nature.

Perhaps understandably, the country also enjoyed a strong temperance movement. An entire voting bloc of exasperated womenfolk flooded the ballots after independence and voted in Prohibition (*Kieltolaki*), which lasted from 1919 to 1932. As in America, this led to a culture of secret drinking, 'fortified' teas and cross-border bootlegging. Booze was sneaked in from Tallinn and Danzig (Russia and Sweden, each for different reasons, not offering much of a supply), and by the 1920s, 80% of reported Finnish 'crime' was linked to the supply or consumption of alcohol. In 1930, one year's confiscated alcohol amounted to over a million litres. A 1931 referendum voted by an overwhelming majority to repeal the law, but its echoes endure.

Alcohol in Finland remains prohibitively expensive, subject to the guilt tax common to Nordic countries. Harder liquor and wines are only available from the government-run off-licences, which are called Alko without a scrap of irony – it is short for *Alkoholiliike*, or State Alcohol Monopoly. As with Finnish restaurants, these establishments are usually staffed by ridiculously knowledgeable and experienced connoisseurs, gritting their teeth as they have to ID yet another trio of giggling teenagers trying to buy three litres of cider.

Far from discouraging drinking among the Finns, such obstacles have backfired in many cases, fostering an environment that encourages binge drinking and surreptitious under-the-table tipples. Many otherwise-educated Finnish youths barely encounter alcohol before their twenties, and then have no clue how to use it responsibly. The German tradition of copious, extremely light beer strikes the Finn as a waste of time and effort (alcohol content below 2% remained legal during Finnish Prohibition, and apparently wasn't good enough). Do not be surprised if you hear Finns speaking of a *pre-party* or a *continuation-party*, referring to a booze-up in a private home to get properly munted, as opposed to the official public gathering in a bar or club, where nobody can afford to buy too many drinks. As in other Nordic countries, the concept of 'getting a round in' is regarded as an alien extravagance.

Many Finnish establishments conflate multiple styles of bar into a single venue. It is entirely feasible to walk into a French-style coffee bar (which also serves alcohol – a tobacco-free *tabac*), and pass through inner doors into a snug facsimile of a British pub, and then through further doors to a riotous American-style dive bar (called in Finnish a *räkälä*, or 'place of snot').

Do not be surprised if a passive-aggressive temperance afflicts staff in some restaurants, such as the waitress in Jyväskylä who once asked the author if he 'was sure' he wanted a second beer at lunch. I also report the following guessing game, verbatim, from one of Tampere's best-known hotels.

'And what would sir like to drink?'

'There are no beers on the menu. Presumably you have some?'

'We've got all of them.'

'Fine, I'll have a Guinness.'

'We haven't got that.'

'A Lapin Kulta?'

'We haven't got that, either.'

Despite such obstructions, the visitor is liable to encounter several Finnish beers, whose stories are often more worthy of attention than their flavours. Common brands include **Lapin Kulta** (Gold of Lapland, Lapland Darling), which takes its name from its original brewery in Tornio, although now it is only brewed far to the south, **Karhu** (Bear), and **Koff** (short for the brewer's name, Sinebrychoff). Look out for some odder names, such as Olvi's grab for the military market with **Tuntematon Sotilas** (the Unknown Soldier, named for Väinö Linna's novel), and **Sandels**, named for Count Johan August Sandels (1764–1831), who led Swedish troops to victory against the Russians in the Finnish War – he won the battle, but lost the war. History also comes to the fore with **Karjala** (Karelia), which uses the coat of arms of Karelia as its logo. This presents the armoured sword-arm of a European knight striking a blow against a scimitar-wielding Asian. The brand was losing market share until the 1960s, when the Soviet ambassador complained that it evoked echoes of the Winter War. Finns immediately began quaffing it in great quantities. The Laitila brewery produces a variety of ales, including the pointlessly strong **Imperiaali**, a black, gloopy poison at 9.2%, adorned with a double-headed rooster, spoofing the Tsar's crest of old. Other common beers in Finland include Estonian brands such as **A. le Coq** and **Saku**.

European Union regulations decree that Finnish grain alcohols be termed *vodka*, although locally the Russian word is usually only applied to imported liquors. Locally, grain alcohol is often called *viina*, or in Swedish, *bränvinn*. The most famous brand is **Koskenkorva** (or more affectionately, *Kossu*), which forms the basis of many modern, quaintly bonkers Finnish cocktails. These include the *Kossukola* (with Coke), the Kossu Battery (with an energy drink), and the Fisu (with crushed Fisherman's Friend cough lozenges). Particularly popular among visitors, and sold in ready-made bottles, is **Salmiakki Koskenkorva** (popularly nicknamed Salmiakki Kossu or Salmari), which combines a famous local *viina* with Turkish Pepper flavouring. The result is a jet-black vodka that tastes of liquorice. It makes for a fine souvenir, although the appeal soon wears off – many are the enthusiastic converts who never finish the bottle they bring home.

Among unique Finnish tipples, the historically-minded traveller's attention is drawn to **Marskin Ryyppy** (the Marshal's Schnapps), a mixture of strong alcohol, vermouth and a touch of gin, allegedly concocted by Mannerheim's adjutant during the Winter War as a means of coping with low-quality rotgut. It smells and tastes like a mad scientist has been trying to recreate a vodka martini in a lab, and is served judderingly ice-cold in shots. The glasses are customarily filled to overflowing, so that a meniscus of alcohol peaks over the top. Depending on who you ask, this is either a relic of the Russian Chevalier Guard, who wanted to ensure their mandated single shot a day had the maximum content, or of Mannerheim's wartime custom of watching his officers as they drank, and furloughing anyone whose jangled nerves led them to spill a drop.

Finland's other claim to fame (or infamy) in the alcohol stakes came into being in 1952, when the country was barely a generation out of Prohibition, but facing the prospect of a vast influx of foreign tourists coming to the Helsinki Olympics. Enterprising bar-owners, pressed for storage space and disposal logistics, hit on the idea of mixing vats of hard liquor with gallons of flavoured soda, in order to make bulk quantities of what might be termed alcopops in other countries. In Finland they were known as 'long drinks,' popularly shortened to *lonkero*, which literally means 'tentacle'. The most popular brand dilutes perfectly good gin with acrid, sharp grapefruit juice – as with the Marskin Ryypy, it seems like an *imitation*, in this case as if an infant school had been left in charge of creating a facsimile of a gin and tonic. The author is baffled, and eternally exasperated, as to why *Finland didn't just mix the gin with tonic*.

Finland has taken several hesitant steps into the world of whisky, although currently it is more of a waiting game. **Panimoravintola Beer Hunters** in Pori is waiting for its first malt casks to mature in 2034, while **Panimoravintola Koulu** in Turku released a three-year-old malt in 2013. **Teerenpeli's** six-year-old single malt was released in Lahti in 2009 – every bottle comes with a free wooden coaster, as well it might at €70 for half a litre.

8

Travel Logistics

FINNISH WINTERS, of course, are notoriously cold, but the country is ready for them and handles snow and ice with infinitely better preparation and efficiency than Britain. An entire infrastructure of snow-movers and gritters keeps the country running smoothly in Arctic conditions, along with smart innovations like heated runways and high streets, and compulsory snow tyres.

Finnish summers, particularly once the sun is up for most of the night, can get hot. Don't get caught out in June like Mrs Tweedie in *Through Finland in Carts*:

Our hostess's first exclamation when we arrived at her beautiful country home was an inquiry as to the contents of the large hold-all.

'Rugs,' we replied, 'and fur coats.'

'Rugs and fur coats,' she exclaimed in amusement. 'What for?'

'To wear, of course,' we answered.

'Did you think Finland was cold, then?' she asked.

'Certainly,' we returned, 'so we have each brought a rug and a fur-lined coat.'

She laughed and said, 'Far better to have brought cotton frocks.'

It was our turn now to be amazed, and we asked her what she meant by cotton frocks.

'Why, do you not know that our summer is much hotter than it is in England – it is shorter, but much warmer.'

Finland is a European Union country, and has visa-free access for EU members. Visitors planning a jaunt over the Gulf of Finland to Estonia should remember it, too, is an EU country. However, it is substantially harder for the visitor to simply jump on a train to Russia, as many Finns seem to do. Depending on the political climate, UK travellers planning a trip to Russia will often have to apply for their visas in advance at home, and have them already in their passports when they arrive in Helsinki.

The country was an enthusiastic early adopter of the euro. Finnish ATMs are trilingual, take foreign cards, and usually switch automatically to English-language operation when they detect a card's origin. However, some sales points, such as the automated ticket machines in Finnish railway stations, do *not* accept foreign cards – get your ticket from a human.

Although the Finnish post is very efficient and reliable, neither it nor its post offices function on weekends – a hard-fought concession won by the labour union in the 1970s. Stamps and minor postal services can, however, be bought at R-Kioski convenience stores. If you are going to be asking them to weigh your letters, try not to do it at five on a Saturday when everyone else is queuing for their Lotto tickets.

Finnish public transport is sternly exact in its time-keeping – nobody wants to wait an extra minute at the bus stop when the temperature is minus 15, and buses and trains reflect this punctuality. In winter, do as the Finns do and lurk indoors till the last possible moment. In concession to the faff required to get change out of pockets and hold tickets in gloved hands, there are often no ticket gates on the Helsinki metro. There are, however, ticket inspectors on the trains themselves, so remember to buy your ticket before boarding.

To hear some Finns talk about their railway system, you would be forgiven for thinking it was a third-world shambles, but they have clearly never been to Britain. Finnish trains are a paradise of comfort and efficiency, and distinguished by some neat touches like free travel for any children accompanied by an adult (including teenagers, hence reducing the numbers of unaccompanied louts), children's carriages with their own play rooms, and free travel for any off-duty police who wear their uniforms, ensuring a little bit of bonus security. If you are sure of your dates, you can book online in English at www.vr.fi and explore a plan of your train, to determine whether it has a bike rack, pram park, smoking room or pet corner. Finnish Pendolino trains, however, can occasionally freeze up in the cold. Finns take some pride in pointing out that this was because they were designed by Italians.

Many Finnish towns have a local airport, which can trim hours off journeys. However, be aware that when it comes to air travel, almost all roads lead to Helsinki, which lies in the far south. If you wish to travel by plane from, say, Jyväskylä to Tampere, the time wasted by flying south to Helsinki, changing planes, and then heading out north again cancels any speed benefit over simply taking the train.

National Holidays and Local Festivals

Finnish national holidays largely reflect those of the Christian world, with occasional oddities left over from the distant pagan past. There are also several flag days on which it is legally mandated to fly the Finnish flag. These include 28th February (Finnish Culture day, also *Kalevala* Day), Vappu (see below), Mother's Day, 4th June (Mannerheim's birthday, also Finnish Defence Forces Day), Juhannus (see below), and election days. Some unofficial days have also become flaggable, such as Father's Day, Swedes' Day, Finnish (Language) Day and several celebrities' birthdays. However, in no case does any of the above flag-waving signify any closures of shops or alterations to transport schedules.

Epiphany (Loppiainen)

The 6th January is also a national holiday in Finland. Shopping is usually impossible. The fact that the Epiphany holiday is also liable to coincide with the Eastern Orthodox Christmas means that many Russians are on holiday, and liable to pile onto the train from St Petersburg.

Easter (Pääsiäinen)

The Finnish Easter retains elements of the country's Russian past, as well as traditions from pagan Karelia. *Mämmi* (see Eating and Drinking) is consumed, as is *pasha*, a creamy delight that takes its name from the Russian for Easter, and is a suitable high-calorie celebration of the end of a Lenten fast.

The gap between Good Friday and Easter Sunday is supposedly the point in the year where God's power is weakest, leading to many legends of witches and trolls. In a custom not dissimilar to trick-or-treating, children are apt to go door-to-door dressed as witches and waving twigs as wands, chanting a spell in Finnish so archaic that it is practically Estonian:

> *Virvon, varvon*
> *tuoreeks terveeks,*
> *tulevaks vuodeks,*
> *ison talon emännäks.*
> *Vitsa sulle,*
> *palkka mulle.*

In the unlikely event the visitor is confronted with such a supernatural assault, the words imply that a nice house and long life is assured if you bribe them with sweets. If you do not want a nice house and long life, slam the door in their face and face sorcerous consequences.

Vappu (Walpurgisnacht)

The Nordic summer is notoriously short, and the Finns, like other northern races, are aggressively keen to wring the most out of it as possible. Finns go certifiably mental on the evening of the 30th April and day of 1st May, in what is supposedly a series of ceremonies to mark Labour Day, but usually little more than excuse for a party. The more genteel Finns will picnic in the park and sip on low-alcohol mead (*sima*). But the day really belongs to the students, who are liable to rampage through town centres wearing boiler-suits festooned with sponsor patches. Anyone who has graduated from a Finnish high school dons their white graduation cap on this day, which makes many Finnish towns look like they have been over-run with sailors. The celebrations officially begin at 6pm on 30th April, when one such cap will be jauntily placed on the head of the statue of Havis Amanda (see Gazetteer: Helsinki).

Juhannus (St John's Eve)

As with Vappu in the spring, Finland's midsummer celebration of St John's Eve on 22nd June has less to do with any prosaic or modern events, and owes more to an atavistic, primal celebration of summer itself. Its origins seem to date back to the pagan festival of Ukko, the chief god of Finland's pantheon, who was worshipped with great pyres.

Finns are liable to run to the countryside in summer anyway, and will be all the more absent from town centres on this day – it usually amounts to a three-line whip for family gatherings, analogous to the American Thanksgiving, and often seems to exert more of a gravitational pull than even Christmas. Midsummer is hence the time when the Finnish infrastructure is most likely to grind to a halt – don't expect to find anything open except the occasional kebab shop and a corner store that has run out of barbecue sausages.

Finns are deeply proud of their summer cottages, and midsummer is arguably the best time to experience them, swimming in a lake after a wood-fired sauna, beneath a never-ending sunset. Finns frolic in the woods, get drunker than usual, and light massive bonfires that they insist on calling *kokko*, even in English, even though there is no discernable difference between a *kokko* and any other pile of wood set upon by pyromaniacs. As it is also Finnish Flag Day, many country cottages have a flagpole, where the blue-and-white pennant is raised with a degree of ceremony. This is also the only day where the flag stays up all night, in honour of the fact that the night itself is very short, or in the north, practically non-existent.

Many pagan rituals persist in modern folklore, including the superstition that a maiden who collects seven different flowers and sleeps with them under her pillow will dream of her future husband. Will-o'-wisps are said to lead pure-hearted forest wanderers to buried treasure, and a virgin who bends naked over a well is supposed to see her future husband's face in the water. You'll have to make your own jokes here, as my editor vetoed mine.

All Saints' Day (Pyhäinpäivä)

The plastic-pumpkin Americanised Halloween is slowly destroying any uniquely Finnish traditions. The more devout Finns will scurry to the local cemetery and place windproof candles on the graves of relatives and friends. Particularly on the nearest Saturday to Halloween, the lit graveyards can look hauntingly beautiful in the autumn darkness.

Some Finnish farm towns used to assemble a ram effigy in fir or wicker branches, dragging it through the streets and burning it (sometimes on a nearby lake) on All Saint's Day as a form of post-harvest festival. Known as a *Kekripukki*, the name literally means 'relict ram', although early Christian commentators suggested that Kekri was a homonym for a forgotten fertility god, and also a term for the end of the agricultural year. Kekripukki celebrations, which also included mummery, costumed antics and wassailing, were viewed as deeply suspect by the early Church. Its siting on All Saints' Day appears to have been a Christian attempt to incorporate it within the Church year, whereas different locales previously held their celebrations on slightly different autumn dates. The tradition faded out in modern times, lingering for a while in Eastern Finland. Modern Kekripukki celebrations can still be found in Oulu and Kajaani.

Christmas Eve (*Jouluaatto*)

Like many Europeans, the Finns celebrate Christmas on the night before Christmas Day, which they call *Joulu*, cognate with the Norse Yule. Santa Claus (*Joulupukki*) may put in a live appearance, although he usually manages to arrive whenever Dad has popped out to the cornershop. As a result, the two of them are suspiciously rarely seen together – the alert visitor can often look out the window and see several Santas at once stumbling through the snow from house to house in the afternoon, as neighbours swap Santa responsibilities. Many Finns also take candles to the cemetery, thereby getting rid of any spares leftover from All Saints' Day.

New Year (*Uusi Vuosi*)

In what seems to be a relic of a Karelian smithy tradition, some Finns heat tin scraps and then fling the molten metal into a bucket of water. The flash-hardened residue is then examined for shapes, portents, images and omens of the future. This will be what a Finn means when he tells you he has been at a party, 'examining slags'.

9

Gazetteer

'CAN YOU IMAGINE, when I was in Finland they took me to see an 18th-century wooden church,' scoffed Silvio Berlusconi, that one-man anti-Finland missile. 'I remember how important this was to them. We woke up early in the morning and travelled to the church for three hours. Over here such a church would have been bulldozed to the ground.'

Berlusconi's aghast reaction is repeated here for the awful image it presents of southern European dignitaries' unrealistic expectations, and the Finns' earnest but vain efforts to impress them. It is, of course, gauche and inconsiderate of Berlusconi to expect objects in Finland of a similar culture and type to those he is used to in his ruin-clogged homeland. Finland's harsh environment and harsher recent history has done for many stone buildings and ancient relics, but it is helpful to recall that much of Finland's appeal, ever since the first travellers arrived on a Grand Tour, has been its unspoilt nature.

Berlusconi will never be able to look up into Italian night skies, as visitors to Lapland can so often do, and see the ghostly green river of the Aurora Borealis shimmering in the crisp air, making castles of light and sparkling wild hunts of phantoms. He cannot trudge through an Italian forest that stretches for hundreds of miles, or jet-ski a whole eighteen-hour day along the coasts of a lake that cuts through the middle of his country. It is unlikely that he will enjoy the mad thrill of taking a shortcut to work across a frozen river, although one presumes it is all too likely that he has, at some point, been whipped with birch twigs by a naked girl in a steamy room. In summary, while history is the main interest of this book, travellers to Finland itself should also take the time to smell the flowers, swat the mosquitoes and appreciate the view. I have hard-heartedly neglected to mention many sites' undeniable natural beauty. For many visitors (and locals), part of the appeal of the country lies in its thousands of square miles of fir trees and birch, dotted by glittering lakes. Finns are likely to be crestfallen that I haven't mentioned 'the lovely lake and fine trees' near a particular town, although since that largely describes every town in the land, the reader should take it as given.

Finland prides itself on an immense amount of tiny regional museums, with practically any local figure who achieves anything even remotely of note sure to get at least a room in the local library laid out in their honour. Noting the presence of a scale model of the town in the town museum, an otherwise unremarkable art collection, an old boat in the harbour, or a statue of a Finnish president in the village square, is not really an indulgence that can be permitted in a book of this concise nature. The reader should also take it as given that any town centre boasts an old church and an earnest museum recreating some element of How We Used to Live, often situated in some authentic burgher's house. Seen one, seen 'em all, unless otherwise noted below.

I tender my apologies in advance to those many small museums or tourist sites in less prominent townships that are unlikely to excite the interest of the casual tourist, and which I have regrettably had to leave out. The reader in search of a more minute examination of places of interest in rural and suburban Finland is directed to *Finland: A Cultural Guide*, by Louhenjoki-Schulman and Hedenström, which has far more space to do such places justice.

In keeping with Finnish orthography, the letters Å, Ä and Ö come at the *end* of the alphabet. Titles give the Finnish name first and Swedish name second – this would be reversed if this were an appendix to an armchair traveller's history of Sweden. For the appendix on the 'Lost Lands' now part of Russia, the modern Russian name is given first, with the former Finnish name in parentheses.

Ahvenanmaa (Åland)

Finnish by decree, Swedish by nature, the Åland Islands in the Baltic Sea are the only part of the country to have a single official language – Swedish. The fact that the islands are Finnish at all can largely be attributed to the careful diplomacy of Mannerheim during his brief regency, but originally also to the Russian era, when Tsar Alexander I coveted a naval base in the middle of the Baltic, and insisted that they were part of his Grand Duchy. Alexander made a bold architectural statement with the **Eckerö Mail and Customs House**, a ludicrously ostentatious building, deliberately designed to mark the point where Russian territory began for the benefit of all those passing ships. Nicholas I built more practical edifices to protect his western reaches, which survive today as the **Bomarsund Fortification Ruins** near Sund– blown up by the British and French in 1854. It was here that Tsar Alexander III once supposedly had an embarrassing encounter with a local official, who caught him netting crayfish out of season. Not recognising the poacher, the official berated him for being an ignorant toff, and departed still hurling epithets, while the red-faced emperor tipped his catch back into the sea. At least that is the story; it is similar to many Swedish folktales about earlier rulers, which makes the author suspicious.

Although there are over 6,000 Åland islands, visitors without their own ship are liable to see just Mariehamn (Marie's Harbour), the capital and site of the biggest marina in Scandinavia. Named for Alexander II's wife, Mariehamn supplanted the old centre of Åland life, **Kastelholm** (Island Castle) in Sund, which looks disappointingly like a couple of warehouses from a distance, but nevertheless has a rich, royal history told within its walls. Tsar Alexander III's favourite spot was actually the barren rocks of **Geta** in the north of the islands, where he used to walk, contemplating the stony brink of his domain.

Åland Maritime Museum commemorates the islands' heyday as a sailing hub, and preserves the four-masted windjammer *Pommern*. Built in Scotland in 1903, she was transporting grain from Australia to Britain until the outbreak of WW2. The museum contains many other items of interest, salvaged from long-gone clippers and barques, including a rare *male* ship's figurehead.

Alavus

The site of the historical **Battle of Alavus** (1808), the highpoint of Swedish success against Russia in the Finnish War, Alavus is on the map today for more modern associations. Situated in the nearby village of Tuuri is **Keskinen Brothers**, a vast shopping centre dedicated to the ethos of piling it high and selling it cheap. The complex is clad to look like a medieval castle for no discernable reason, and includes a hotel, campsite, several restaurants and a giant horseshoe, memorably described by one website as the **Third Worst Building in the World**. As if this were not enough of a claim to fame, eccentric millionaire Vesa Keskinen has scattered the adjacent park with statues of unicorns. Keskinen is certainly a showman who knows what sort of artefacts and activities are liable to lure Finns over for the weekend – if you want to see **Lordi's Eurovision-winning mask**, it is hanging up in the music department. The Finnish Tourist Board states, through gritted teeth, that the whole site is the most popular tourist attraction in Finland, perhaps confusing the obvious allure of discount shopping with the performance of cultural pursuits. There's usually plenty for the kids to do while mum snags a bulk order of toilet paper, which helps tempt over six million annual visitors to this remote location – although such figures presumably include 52 visits a year from each and every local who pops in to buy a packet of mince.

Askainen (Villnäs)

Baron Hermann Clausson Fleming (1619–1673) was a prominent Swedish noble, ousted by court politics and handed the poison chalice that was the governorship of Finland. He cheered himself up by building the stout, square house of **Louhisaari Manor** in the 1660s by the sea, although the coastline has silted up somewhat since his day. This would be otherwise unremarkable, were it not for the house's later acquisition by the Mannerheim family, whose most famous son was born at Louhisaari in 1867. Today, the manor house is a museum to both the Flemings and the Mannerheims, artfully combining elements of the Swedish and Russian eras, as well as a glimpse of the childhood of a Finnish president. The young Gustaf Mannerheim's playhouse is preserved in the grounds. But you can't play in it.

Espoo (Esbo)

Once a manor on the King's Road to the east, now little more than a conjoined twin of Helsinki, Espoo most often turns up on travellers' itineraries because the hotels there are cheaper than the nearby capital, which is only a bus-ride away. The Wee-Gee Building, once the site of a printing press, plays host to both the **Espoo City Museum** and the **Helinä Rautavaara Museum**, dedicated to the clutter and artefacts brought back by the eponymous journalist (1928–1998), who wrote about foreign cultures for 40 years. Of greater interest in terms of the broad sweeps of Finnish nationalism is the **Gallen-Kallela Museum**, based in the artist's old studio, which he designed himself with typical idiosyncratic flourishes.

Helsinki (Helsingfors)

Although certain Finns may grumble (see Gazetteer: Turku), and locals themselves sometimes whine about their capital as if it were some sort of urban jungle, Helsinki is a charming city. Architects feted elsewhere in their Finnish hometowns have left many of their finest marks in the very buildings of the central district. Many of its sites are within walking distance, and a tourist bus line links the outliers and the cruise ship terminal. Buses and quaint trams ply similar routes, including one tram that is a travelling pub. Visitors should be warned: it lacks a travelling toilet.

The visitor's first sight of Helsinki, either descending from the airport bus or arriving by train, is liable to be **Rautatientori** (Railway Square), dominated by the temple-like railway station designed by Eliel Saarinen, its walls held aloft by great stone titans like heavy-metal rock gods. Animated and rendered a little cuter, these colossi often appear on posters and adverts for VR, the Finnish rail network. The author admits to a dorky thrill whenever he arrives at the station, as often one will catch a glimpse of the St Petersburg train at one of the platforms, adorned with alien Cyrillic, staffed by scowling *baboushkas*, and ready to depart for another world.

In the square outside the station's east exit, outside the vampire's castle that is the **National Theatre**, an odd statue of the author and playwright Aleksis Kivi shifts uncomfortably in his seat, as if he has just sat on something sticky. He faces the **Ateneum**, Helsinki's National Gallery, and home to many of the most famous artworks of the National Romantic period.

A few steps to the south-west of the square is the southern end of Mannerheimintie, (Mannerheim Road), named for the country's famous Regent and one-time President. This is the centre of Helsinki's shopping district, boasting an iconic statue of blacksmiths at work, and the entrance to the Stockmann department store that sits beneath the **Stockmann Clock**. There is nothing particularly remarkable about the clock, but Finns seem to cling to it as a meeting place, and an encounter 'beneath the Stockmann clock' is an early phrase that torments many beginning students of Finnish.

The **Statue of Mannerheim** on his horse is here, walking earnestly *past* the nearby parliament, rather than facing it or putting his back to it. Statues of other Finnish presidents lurk around the parliament steps like discombobulated party guests, staring dourly at the news crews shooting pick-ups, and across the road at **Kiasma**, the modern-art counterpart to the Ateneum.

With typical Finnish self-awareness, the **Suomen Kansallismuseo** (National Museum of Finland) is itself a museum exhibit, one wing of which is designed to look like a church, which stood it in good stead during the war, when its appearance may have warded off Russian bombers. It was also the site of some scuffles during the Finnish Revolution, and its front doors still proudly display the bullet holes shot in the windows, now preserved behind a second layer of glass. The lobby is decorated with frescoes depicting scenes from the *Kalevala*, painted by Akseli Gallen-Kallela, and that's before you've even bought your ticket!

Russian-era Helsinki was famously designed in imitation of St Petersburg, leading to its substitution for that city as a film location during the Cold War. Although tour guides make much of this, anyone who has seen St Petersburg themselves will know that the resemblance is merely superficial. Watch one of the aforesaid films, such as Warren Beatty's *Reds* (1981), and images of Helsinki are shot in close-up, offering little more than street-level backgrounds and cobbled streets. Commonly, 'St Petersburg' imagery in films derives from **Senaatintori** (Senate Square) at the city's historical centre, with towering steps leading up to the Neo-Classical cupolas of **Helsinki Cathedral**. The cathedral is frankly more impressive on the outside than within, since its interior displays an austere Lutheranism, as if Ikea were put in charge of church design. In the centre of the square stands the **Statue of Alexander II**, 'the Good Tsar' who granted the Grand Duchy of Finland greater autonomy under Russia than it had ever enjoyed under Sweden. It is supposedly the only statue of a Tsar standing outside Russia, and is an enduring testament to the love that the Finns once had for the country to the east. As the Russification policies of his successors began to bite, Alexander's statue became the site of a subtle, peaceful protest as Finns laid wreaths at his feet, mourning not only his death, but also the slow erosion of his kind policies.

From Senaatintori it is but a short walk to the cobbled harbour, the site of many a farmer's market and coffee kiosk, and ferries. The site of Helsinki was originally called Vironniemi (Estonia Point), and its proximity to Tallinn is still reflected in the hydrofoil terminal that will whisk you away in just 90 minutes. For anyone who is inexplicably tired of the Finnish capital, Estonia beckons within commuting distance. The harbour sits at the end of the Esplanadi, twinned parallel north and south avenues that lead back to Mannerheimintie, and constitute some of Helsinki's prime real estate – their meeting place, at Erottaja, is the most expensive spot on a Finnish Monopoly board. It is the site of several posh restaurants, the Swedish Theatre, and **Havis Amanda**. This naked nymph, sculpted by Ville Vallgren (see Gazetteer: Porvoo), reflects the artist's Art Nouveau inspirations, and was the subject of scandalised tutting in the Finnish media when unveiled in 1908. A loving recreation of the gamine curves of a French teenager, it caused uproar among Finland's newly enfranchised women voters but is now a much-loved part of the scenery, affectionately nicknamed Manta. Her fountain waters apocryphally grant sexual potency to anyone who thrice washes their face and shouts '*Rakastaa!*' (Love), and her crowning with a white student's cap marks the beginning of Walpurgisnacht celebrations (see National Holidays and Local Festivals: Vappu). What was once clearly a student prank is now televised annually.

The harbour is also the place to get the ferry to nearby **Suomenlinna**, the Fortress of Finland, which remains a quaint getaway for the marine-minded. It evokes the Swedish, Russian and Finnish eras with numerous installations, as well as a couple of military museums and the *Vesikko*, a WW2 submarine open to the public. Visitors can also poke around the largely ruined fortifications – don't miss the **King's Gate**, built in 1752 as a sufficiently royal arrival point for Swedish rulers. Nearby inscriptions note that King Adolf Frederick laid the first stone here, while a sad, uncompleted plaque leaves the date blank for King Gustav's laying of the final stone (he never got around to it). Beneath a plaque announcing that these 'wolf islands' have been transformed into a fort for the Swedes, a second inscription intones these immortal words: '*Eftervärld, stå här på egen botn, och lita icke på främmande hielp.*' It is a fine prophecy for the world that lay in wait for the Finns: 'Those that come after us, stand here on your own foundation, and trust not in foreign help.' Arrive at around 09:30 or 17:15 and you can watch the gigantic cruise ships squeeze through the narrow strait ('Gustav's Sword') to Helsinki harbour.

Helsinki City Museum is not one but eight separate facilities dotted around the city, including several villas and burghers' houses, and the **Street Museum** on Sofiankatu, which recreates town life in earlier times.

The **Uspenski Cathedral**, Orthodox counterpart to the Lutheran one, is a more sedate, red-brick affair, deriving its name from the Russian for 'the Dormition of Mary'. Perhaps Helsinki's most internationally well-known religious building is further out of the centre at the **Tempeliaukion Kirkko** (the Church in the Rock), which as the name implies, was hewn into the bedrock. For some reason, this site appears to attract more than its fair share of Japanese tourists.

Out in the Kaivopuisto district, where many foreign embassies and consulates can still be found, the **Mannerheim Museum** is sited inside the former president's house. Beware: it is only open on Fridays, Saturdays and Sundays, and free-range visitors are not permitted. The admission fee includes a well-informed guide, although only speakers of Finnish, Swedish and English are liable to be available off the cuff. If you speak French, German, Spanish or Russian, it is best to book ahead. Another Finnish president, who defined the nation throughout the Cold War, is celebrated at the **Urho Kekkonen Museum** in Tamminiemi – you can book a guide any time but it is far cheaper to take the once-a-day scheduled English tour at 14:30. Finnish and Swedish tours are far more regular; German ones must be booked in advance.

These are but a fraction of the many sights that one can find in Helsinki, which is riddled with smaller museums celebrating everything from the post office to the power company to the Salvation Army. As one might expect from any capital, it is also richly endowed with living history. You can still have cocktails at the **Hotel Torni**, a favourite hang-out for Cold War spies, or stroll in **Kaisaniemi Park**, where the eleven-year-old Mannerheim won his first recorded victory – a snowball fight. Kaisaniemi is also home to the tranquil botanical gardens; the former Department of Botany building in the garden was once earmarked as the royal palace of the uncrowned King Väinö I (see Chapter 4).

Hämeenlinna (Tavastehus)

The old administrative centre of the marchland of Tavastia, Hämeenlinna still has the red-brick castle that gives the town its name, which is also home to a **Prison Museum**. The town is also the **Birthplace of Sibelius** – the wooden house where this event occurred is now renovated as a museum in the composer's honour.

Iisalmi

Once a famous spa town in the Russian era, Iisalmi is better known today for what it has brought from Russia. The **New Valamo Monastery**, hosting monks from the 'Old' Valaam Monastery on Lake Ladoga, is a centre for Finnish Orthodoxy. The town's **Evacuation Center** (*Evakkokeskus*) tells this story of lost Karelia (see Appendix: The Lost Lands), and is one of the few places in Finland that appears to commemorate the thousands of Finns who fled west at the end of the Second World War. The town is also home to **Kuappi**, the 'world's smallest restaurant', which holds just two people. Probably best to book in advance.

Imatra

'Later, sitting on a rocky boulder, we gazed in awe at the scene before us. This was *Imatra*. This is one of the three famous falls which form the chain of a vast cataract. This avalanche of foam and spray, this swirling, tearing, rushing stream, this endless torrent pursuing its wild course, year in, year out – this was *Imatra*, one of the strongest water powers in the world – the Niagara of Europe.' Mrs Alec Tweedie, *Through Finland in Carts*.

Although things have changed a lot since the construction of the Imatrankoski power plant in 1926, the rapids at Imatra remain the area's main tourist attraction. In a quaint recursion, the tourist attraction has itself become a tourist attraction, with the **Imatra Cultural Centre** listing numerous dignitaries and artists who came to witness the roaring river, from Count Per Brahe, through the painters Edelfelt, Gallen-Kallela and Sparre, Richard Wagner, Alexandre Dumas *père*, and Empress Catherine II. This thriving tourist industry was eventually met in 1903 with the imposing **Valtionhotelli** (State Hotel), built in the National Romantic style, and popularly a honeymoon for Finns before the days of cheap air travel. Perhaps because loud music is the only thing that can be heard above the waters, Imatra also became the centre for the music festival Jokirokki (literally **Rock to the River**) and a **Big Band Festival**, although the former seems now only to be intermittent.

Inari

Siida, better known in English as the Sámi Museum, gives Rovaniemi's Artikum a run for its money. Originally intended as an open-air museum, it is now open plan, set within a vault-like modernist chamber, and telling the story of the peoples of Lapland and their adaptation to its hostile environment. Its exhibits segue nicely into those of the **Northern Lapland Nature Centre** nearby, which tells a similar narrative from the point of view of local botany and biology.

Joensuu

'River Mouth' is close enough to the Russian border to still offer coach tours into Karelia. Its **North Karelian Museum** exhibits many artefacts evacuated from Sortavala, on the shores of Lake Ladoga in what is now Russia (see Gazetteer: the Lost Lands: Sortavala). **Joensuu Art Museum** is uncommonly internationalist, featuring works from as far afield as China.

Jyväskylä

Billing itself as 'the Athens of the North', Jyväskylä might surprise the unwary visitor by looking almost exactly like everywhere else in Finland. But the name derives from the presence of early teaching colleges and academies, not from a surfeit of Greek culture. This university town's biggest draw for tourists from all over the world is its status as the testing bed for many works by the renowned architect Alvar Aalto. Interested parties should head straight for the **Alvar Aalto Museum**, which not only collates his life and work, but will sell you an informative €1 Aaltophile booklet, detailing the locations and stories of many other buildings in town that were his. These include the neighbouring **Museum of Central Finland** and numerous university buildings, and a raft of other sites that might otherwise pass the visitor by. Ever one to micro-manage the environments *around* his designs, Aalto himself would have conniptions at some of the more recent additions to the town, particularly the jumble of buildings and a motorway that now sit between his favourite hillside and the lake view below.

While almost every Finnish town seems to have a summer arts event of some description, Jyväskylä comes to vibrant life for a week every year with **Jyväskylän Kesä** (Jyväskylä's Summer), seemingly encompassing all the arts at once. The streets suddenly fill up with African drummers, capering French violinists, mimes, theatre troupes and bands, but unfortunately so too do the hotels, so book early if planning a cultural overdose.

Kajaani (Kajana)

'Down in front of me was little Kajana, all gaily red and white and brown, in a clearing of pale fields; beyond, east and west, were five great grey lakes and a line of low hills. All over the country lay forest, like a shaggy fell.' So wrote Rosalind Travers of the view in 1908 of a town that briefly flourished a century ago as *the* place to ride the rapids to Oulu in a tar boat – sadly no longer an option available to tourists.

If the town of Kajaani seems oddly passive-aggressive about its most famous resident, Elias Lönnrot, it's because he hated it there. While the author of the *Kalevala* gets a grudging statue near the town centre, the town he described as 'a hole of misery ... where there are two streets: one for pigs in the rain, and another for the rich people on a sunny day,' remains perhaps understandably dismissive of him, like a jilted lover. The author's house was demolished, and the site where once it stood is now a boxy superstore. His birch trees were chopped down, and have been replaced by an off-licence. Similar iconoclasm has struck the ruins of **Kajaani Castle**, a 17th-century fort, blown up by the Russians in 1716. The town added insult to injury by shoving a two-lane highway right through it. This is not quite as bad as it sounds – the castle had previously functioned as a gatehouse over a more modest river crossing – but it has become something of a running joke about the priorities of the locals.

Perhaps realising that this hardly bodes well for the visitor, Kajaani has fought back with *Renfors' Riverside Ramble*, a detailed pamphlet outlining a historical walk around the river bank and over the bridge, taking in many local sites of interest and statues, stretching to a surprising 14 pages of detail and discourse. You can pick it up for free at the tourist centre or the **Kainuu Museum**, a few steps from the train station on Asemankatu.

Despite its small size, Kajaani is the largest urban centre near the ski resort of **Vuokatti** and the spa at **Katinkulta**. It thus attracts a lively herd of shoppers, particularly Russian tourists, and *intermittently* offers some classy tourist goods in its high street. They only seem to resupply once a year, though, so do not be surprised if there is nothing on offer but the usual reindeer and Moomin tat.

Contrary as ever, Mrs Tweedie had nothing but nice things to say about the town, which she noted in *Through Finland in Carts* was 'quiet and sleepy', but where she found the local tar industry bizarrely fascinating. Despite a lifetime of adventure, she pronounced the experience of descending the Oulujoki rapids on a tar boat as 'one of the most exciting experiences imaginable'.

Kokkola (Karleby)

Named for the millionaire who donated the site to the nation, Kokkola's **KH Renlund Museum** proudly tells the tale of the brave locals' bloody-minded resistance to the British Royal Navy during the Crimean War. As evidence, six dead British sailors are buried in the local churchyard, and their captured gunboat is still on display in the town's **English Park**.

Kuhmo

The obscure, compact town of Kuhmo is on the summer events map for hosting the **Kuhmo Chamber Music Festival**. In older times, it happened to be the place where Elias Lönnrot decided on the name *Kalevala* for his collection of old Finnish mythology. The townsfolk have seized upon this factoid, creating the **Juminkeko Centre** celebrating everything to do with Lönnrot and his nation-building poem. Juminkeko is a textbook example of doing multimedia *right*, with a series of fascinating documentaries on call at the dedicated theatre, and an exhibition of the many dozens of foreign editions of the books. Visitors should savour the evident glee with which Kuhmo slags off the nearby town of Kajaani (Lönnrot's actual home), with exhibits that go out of their way to quote every put-down that Lönnrot produced.

The Lönnrot experience reaches its peak in the countryside outside Kuhmo with **Kalevala Spirit**, a living museum that cooks, works and veritably breathes the *Kalevala*. The site recreates a medieval Karelian village, with highly knowledgeable staff on hand to explain technology, culture and customs. Visitors are advised to book ahead, to ensure that a salmon is on the slow-cooking fire, and the smithy is ready for them to try a bit of forging. A hill behind the camp is the resting place of an intricate steampunk *Sampo* – site staff advised on the disappointingly awful Finnish kung-fu movie *Jade Warrior*, the producers of which gave them the movie's version of the *Kalevala* McGuffin as a thank-you. Next door to the Kalevala Spirit site is Kuhmo's informative and wide-ranging **Winter War Museum**.

Kuopio

Founded in the 18th century, this modern city has few residents or events of tourist-attracting note. It is perhaps most famous among educators as the birthplace of the social reformer Minna Canth, a fact seized upon by the recreation of her home in **Old Kupoio Museum**, swiftly done before her adopted hometown of Jyväskylä could lay claim to her. **JV Snellman's Home** is also a museum, dedicated to the 19th-century champion of the Finnish language, but neither of these individuals commands much of an audience outside Finns themselves. That honour arguably goes to the **Orthodox Church Museum of Finland**, which commemorates the pomp and pageantry of the Eastern Orthodox Church, exhibiting many icons liberated from the lost lands of Karelia. Kuopio remains the seat of the Orthodox archbishop of Finland – Helsinki and Oulu are mere dioceses.

Lahti

Named for the 'bay' on which it sits, the southern shore of Laka Päijänne, Lahti is the terminus for the picturesque ten-hour cruise from Jyväskylä. The **Radio and TV Museum** commemorates the first amateur broadcasts in 1924, and the **Ski Museum** tackles its subject with Finnish thoroughness, not only commemorating a bunch of presumably famous sportsmen, but also the role of the ski in Finnish history, from the swift-sliding archers who repelled Viking invaders in the Dark Ages, to the 'White Death' rangers who hounded the Soviets in the Winter War. **Lahti Historical Museum** is noteworthy not only for chronicling the town's story, but also for containing many exhibits evacuated from Viipuri's museum before it fell to the Soviets (see Appendix – The

Lost Lands: Vyborg). Similarly, while almost every town in Finland has an art museum of some description, Lahti's **Art and Poster Museum** goes the extra mile, not only celebrating adverts and propaganda, but also incorporating many works rescued from Viipuri (see also Gazetteer: Lappeenranta for similar relics).

Lappeenranta (Villmanstrand)

Used by Ryanair as an *almost*-Russian airport within EU airspace, Lappeenranta is only 2.5 hours from St Petersburg by coach. Its **Fortress and Cavalry Museum** celebrates the Swedish era, particularly the infamously savage Finnish horsemen who fought in the Thirty Years War. Its proximity to the Russian border made it an ideal site for evacuating treasures from the lost city of Viipuri (see Appendix – the Lost Lands: Vyborg), many of which can be found in the **South Karelian Museum** and the **South Karelian Art Museum** (see also Gazetteer: Lahti for similar relics). Lappeenranta truly flourished after 1856, when the 58-kilometre Saimaa Canal linked the Finnish Lakeland to the Gulf of Finland. The **Canal Museum** is based in an official's former residence, by the side of the old canal. A Saimaa Canal is still in operation, but uses a new channel dug in the 1960s.

Mikkeli (Sankt Michel)

Named for the medieval **Stone Sacristy** (now a church museum) dedicated to the Archangel Michael at nearby Savilahti, Mikkeli seemingly enjoyed a long history as a trading post. The **Suur-Savo Museum** reconstructs the kind of costumes that might have been worn by the owners of 12th century jewellery dug up in nearby Tuukkala, presumably dating from the era of the first northern crusades.

The wartime headquarters of the Finnish army, Mikkeli was heavily bombed as a result, and little of the pre-war town remains. The town celebrates its experience in its coat-of-arms, which today includes the crossed double batons of Gustaf Mannerheim and a Cross of Liberty medal. **Mannerheim's Railway Carriage**, which formed a mobile command post (and once, a tense dining car for Adolf Hitler) sits proudly but a little forlornly on the platform at the railway station. With peeling paint and grimy windows, it is protected by a roof from the rain but not the elements. It is open to visitors only once a year on Mannerheim's birthday, 4th June.

The story of Finland's role in the Second World War is told in detail by the local **Infantry Museum** (*Jalkaväkimuseo*) which does such a thorough job that the nearby **Finnish Headquarters Museum** (*Päämajamuseo*) seems to have rather given up. Installed in the old school requisitioned for Mannerheim's command centre, its exhibits are limited to a pious reconstruction of his offices as they once were, and a room where visitors are expected to sit at computer terminals and navigate multimedia presentations. A far moodier, more evocative experience can be had over the road at 'Seagull' (**Lokki**), a cave hacked out of a cliff, which served as the Finnish communications HQ, and retains much of its fittings.

Naantali (Nådendal)

The 'Valley of Grace', to translate its name, originally referred to nearby Masku, which still has a medieval church. A convent of the Order of St Birgitta was founded there in 1438, but then moved downstream to the coast four years later, to the picturesque town that stole its name. The land was confiscated by the Crown during King Gustav Vasa's grasping reforms, leaving only the **Medieval Convent Church** today. However, the nuns' knitting skills transformed the town into a centre for sock-making. Much of the medieval town burned down long ago, but it retains the winding streets and olde-worlde cottages. A spa and resort during the days of Russian rule, it is better known today as the site of both **Kultaranta** (Golden Beach), the summer residence of the Finnish president, and **Muumimailmaa** (Moomin World) a theme park devoted to the Tove Jansson's Moomins. The picturesque marina, lined with restaurants, offers an element of Mediterranean charm in the summer.

Nurmijärvi

Since it was his novel *Seven Brothers* that put Nurmijärvi on the map, the **Birthplace of Aleksis Kivi**, back when he was plain little Alex Stenvall, has been restored to the conditions it had when he was a child. Nearby **Taaborinvuori** (Tabor Hill) has been turned into one of Finland's infestation of local history museums, and also boasts an open-air theatre where one might hope to catch a performance of a play based on one of Kivi's books.

Oulu (Uleåborg)

Although Oulu officially has a castle, the site is an empty park, the fort itself having been destroyed when a bolt of lightning ignited its gunpowder stores in the 18th century. There's nothing but a café on the old foundations. Otherwise, the amenities conform to more or less every Finnish city's roster of churches, local history museums, albeit with an art museum that focuses on 'north Finnish' art and Sami materials, the 'world's first science centre', and a museum hosting the 'world's oldest diving suit' in nearby Raahe. With pickings so slim, perhaps it's unsurprising that the city is the proud host of the **International Air Guitar Festival** each August.

The statue of the **Market Patrolman** (*Toripolliisi*) by Kaarlo Mikkonen is the result of a rather desperate 1987 attempt to manufacture a local tradition worth celebrating, and is a memorial to the constables who would keep the peace among the traders during the 20th century. The last retired in 1979, and if the statue is anything to go by, spent most of his time at the doughnut stall. Despite the stab at local colour, even to the counter-intuitive double-L spelling which supposedly replicates local dialect, the whole Toripolliisi phenomenon seems archly artificial. The original inspiration for the statue was found in a junk shop in Kajaani, but this doesn't stop Oulu locals trying to push Toripolliisi souvenirs as some sort of unique local phenomenon.

Pietarsaari (Jakobstad)

Pietarsaari Town Museum is disappointingly silent on the town's most notorious appearance in 20th-century newspapers – there is nary a whisper of the Grafton Rifles, and when the author visited in search of them, he was treated instead to a special collections room bafflingly decorated with images of life in modern Greece. Perhaps afraid of being too 'Red' in the White heartland of Ostrobothnia, the site instead favours the culture and antiques of the building's former owner, Peter Malm, a wealthy 19th-century ship-owner.

The town's most unique feature is in on its outskirts, at **The Arctic Museum Nanoq**, a large collection of memorabilia and artefacts from international pioneers of polar exploration and settlement partly set inside an authentic turf-roofed building, along with items of Greenland and Inuit culture. The site of the wreck of the *John Grafton* is marked by a lonely memorial plinth on a remote skerry a few miles out of town (see also Gazetteer: Vaasa).

Pori (Björneborg)

Rebuilt in a florid Italian Renaissance style after a fire of 1852, the port town of Pori is usually recognised for the **Pori Jazz Festival** every summer. Its most imposing Venetian-style building is nicknamed the **Junnelius Palace** by the locals, who tell a story that it was built as a mansion by an eccentric millionaire, who veritably squandered a pile of money sending a relatively lazy and uninspired architect to Italy, where he simply copied a suitable *palazzo* – the design so much a carbon copy that it even has wall-rings for tying up gondolas, despite being on dry land. It was sold to the city by Junnelius's heirs in 1962 and now functions as the New City Hall.

The local **Satakunta Museum** makes a strong case for the region as a flourishing trading site since prehistoric times, and nestles close to the centre, near the theatre, the old city hall and the local brewery. The nearby **Hotel Otava** is now an office building, but was once a hotel, the claim to fame of which was that its dining hall saw what was supposedly the first ever performance of a piece of Finnish-language theatre in 1872. It also served as a headquarters for the Luftwaffe during the Continuation War.

The Neo-Gothic **Juselius Mausoleum**, designed by Josef Stenbäck at the turn of the twentieth century, commemorates the tragic death of 11-year-old Sigrid Juselius, daughter of a local bigwig. It is notable today for its dour, gloomy frescoes by Akseli Gallen-Kallela, including a famous painting of children watching a boy shoot a bird with a crossbow, while a woman in black stares out of the frame. Life, with all its casual brutality, goes on in this picture, uncaring of the grief felt by the bereaved. It's a very Finnish observation, although supposedly not the artist's intention – the picture is supposed to make you think that life goes on in a *good* way, although how this is best illustrated by an image of a miserable little boy killing an animal, your guess is as good as mine.

Porvoo (Borgå)

Described in 1813 by George Green as 'a tolerably good town', Porvoo has retained the cobbled streets and shed-like shacks of its Old Town, where other Finnish cities have cleared them away to make space for another supermarket. The **Edelfelt-Vallgren Museum**, next to the **Historical Museum** in the town centre, celebrates two of the town's most famous sons. Albert Edelfelt (1854–1905) was the most famous Finnish painter of his day, and continued to spend his summers in Porvoo, while being feted the rest of the year in Paris. His Porvoo studio is also open to the public. The sculptor Ville Vallgren (1855–1940) was another local who spent most of his time in France, but is best known in Finland as the creator of Havis Amanda (see Gazetteer: Helsinki). The **Home of JL Runeberg** (1804–1877), poet and author of the national anthem (see Publishers and Authors), has been a museum for over a century, and is just down the road from his son's house, now the **Walter Runeberg Sculpture Collection**. The otherwise unremarkable **Hörbersgården Museum** on Pellinki Island incorporates the summer cabin of Tove Jansson, creator of the Moomins. **Eugen Schauman**, the assassin of Governor-General Bobrikov, is buried in Porvoo cemetery – not even the Finns can bring themselves to raise a statue to a suicidal terrorist, but the man who was once interred in an unmarked grave now rests in his family tomb, which has been built over with a suitably massive and monumental slab.

Punkaharju

In a land that largely comprises lakes and trees, a **Forest Museum** might sound like a step too far. But Punkaharju is on the map for local tourists because of a nearby site of famous natural beauty, where a ridge, all but drowned between two lakes, creates a snaking wooded esker that stretches for miles, barely wider than the road that runs along it. Even Mrs Tweedie liked it:

> Punkaharju is certainly a strange freak of Nature. Imagine
> a series of the most queerly-shaped islands all joined

together by a natural roadway, for, strange to say, there is a ridge of land sometimes absolutely only the width of the road joining these islands in a connective chain. For about five miles these four or five islands are bound together in this very mysterious manner, so mysterious, in fact, that it seems impossible, as one walks along the roadway, to believe it is nature's freak and not man's hand that has made this extraordinary thoroughfare. It is most beautiful in the wider parts, where, there being more land, the traveller comes upon lovely dells, while the most marvellous mosses and ferns lie under the pine trees, and the flowers are beautiful.

Her ability to enjoy the spot was at least partly the result of the first imperial Russian decree on conservation, when Tsar Alexander I visited the site and ordered that it be protected from development. Punkaharju subsequently developed something of a fandom for the Tsars, and hopefully built an imperial annex to the local state hotel, hoping for a visit from Tsar Nicholas II. He never came.

Beyond the famous sight, there is little else in Punkaharju, but local lore holds that its trees and like views are generally nicer than the average, and the forest museum gives visitors another excuse to linger. For many Finnish families, forestry is sure to loom as a profession somewhere back in the family tree.

The **Retretti Art Museum**, housed underground in caves, was once a major feature of Punkaharju, but went bankrupt in 2012 and, at time of writing, has yet to be reopened.

Rovaniemi

The elements and, latterly, the Lapland War of 1944–1945 have ensured that there are no buildings more than 60 years old in Lapland. Rovaniemi has fought back with a passionately modernist engagement with the tourist trade, most famously with **Santa Claus Village**, a theme park that has single-handedly put the town on many international travellers' itineraries. It is eight kilometres outside of town, next to **Santapark**, an underground amusement park, which should not be confused with the village itself. The town is also home to the wonderful arched colonnade that leads to **Arktikum – The Provincial Museum of Lapland and the Arctic Centre**, a museum that deftly balances a narrative of human settlement in Lapland with more scientific exhibits on local biology, botany and geography. Some 19 kilometres outside of Rovaniemi in Norvajärvi, seemingly almost as carefully forgotten as it is possible to be, lies a cemetery of German soldiers.

The town achieved a more ephemeral fame as the home of Lordi, the cheerfully bombastic, grotesquely masked heavy metal band that swept to Eurovision glory in 2006, quite possibly as the result of pan-European student larks. Do not be surprised if you are treated to the band's anthem, 'Hard Rock Hallelujah', at least once during your stay. Lordi fever veritably gripped Finland for a number of years, and led to the renaming of the town's central Sampo Square as Lordi's Square (**Lordin aukio**). The band members' hand prints are preserved in cement here.

Savonlinna (Nyslott)

'The castle of Savo' takes its name from St Olaf's Castle (**Olavinlinna**), the northernmost extant castle of the medieval period, built in 1475 to defend new settlements in the east of Finland, and named Nyslott ('New Castle') in Swedish. With canny calculation, it is actually some way inland, protecting not the old border with Russia itself, but a vital communications nexus that any invading army would be sure to cross. Mrs Alec Tweedie stayed there in the 1890s, spending a night haunted by the ghosts of times past:

Here was the hall of the knights, a long and dark chamber – so dark, in fact, that we wondered how any one had ever been able to see clearly in it. On all sides were rooms and pitch-black dungeons, for at the time the Castle was built (1475) the powers-that-were thought nothing of shutting people up in dark little holes, where they left them to die, and the *Olavin Linna* seems to have been particularly rich in such choice chambers. From where we stood, a few steps up a winding staircase led us to a big tower containing a large round room, called the ladies' drawing-room. The dames of that period certainly had a glorious view all round for miles and miles, although they were far removed from the life going on below. From this point of vantage we saw how the Castle literally covered the whole of the rock, and occupied a most commanding position where three lakes met. As we wandered down again, we chanced into a queer sort of chamber, wherein half a dozen weird straggling trees struggled to exist. It was almost dark; the storms of winter could rustle through those blank windows, and the trees were white, and gray, and sickly – more like phantoms than real trees – so queer and withered and pale and anæmic were their leaves, and yet they stood eight or ten feet high, showing they had boldly struggled for life.

The castle remains an impressive sight, its cold conditions reflected in roofed turrets with portholes instead of crenels. Its chapel is notable in particular for a *hagioscope* – a peephole through which uninvited outsiders could watch a service without disturbing the congregation. This is thought to reflect the presence of lepers in the family of one of the architects. The castle and town come alive in July, when they host the **Savonlinna Opera Festival**, with international class performances in the courtyard. Thanks to the interconnected nature of Finland's lakes, it is possible to get a boat from Savonlinna all the way to Helsinki, via the Saimaa Canal (see Gazetteer: Lappeenranta).

Sonkajärvi

There is nothing to put Sonkajärvi on the map, which is probably why since 1997 it has become the annual home of the Finnish **Wife-Carrying Championship**. The winner takes home his wife's weight in beer. If you aren't married or your spouse is not interested, it is possible to borrow someone else's, but only for the duration of the race.

Tampere (Tammerfors)

Tampere has become an unexpected travel hub in recent years, as it is Ryanair's chosen airport, and hence the likely place of entry for many budget travellers disembarking in misery and discomfort. It has hence gained a better footfall of tourists simply by being the first or last place they see in Finland, and has embraced this role with a number of classy museums.

Proudly, if a little unironically, describing itself as 'the Manchester of the North', Tampere is a hub of modern tourist sites, often steeped in its industrial past. The Finlayson company still produces local textiles, more likely to be found with a Marimekko or Moomin print in modern times. A pleasant stroll from the main train station takes in not only the main shopping street, but also the Hämeensilta bridge across the Tammer rapids – adorned with Wäinö Aaltonen's four statues of ancient life in the area: the Hunter, the Finnish Maiden, the Tradesman and the Tax Collector – to the **Central Square**, which remains a charming example of Jugend style. Built long after Finlayson had left Finland, and hence named for the company rather than the man, the **Finlaysonin Palatsi** (literally *palace*) is an impressive mansion at the water's edge, commissioned by the factory-owning Nottbeck family in 1899. It was converted to a posh restaurant in the 1980s.

Tampere Cathedral is a typically Finnish oddity, designed in the National Romantic style by Lars Sonck (1870–1956), and decorated inside by the certifiably eccentric Hugo Simberg (1873–1917), whose frescoes included a 'Garden of Death', in which cowled skeletons tend roses, and the twelve apostles appear as naked little boys. A massive altarpiece supposedly depicts the resurrection of Lazarus, although it more closely resembles a man emerging from a sauna. Most famously of all, tucked away in a corner you will find 'The Wounded Angel', a depiction of a blindfolded, winged girl on a stretcher, being borne away by two sheepish boys, said to symbolise Finland's battered history stuck between Russia and Sweden.

Foreign visitors are largely spared any engagement with the city's violent upheavals in Finland's civil war, although there are still clues, such as the fact that the town's statue of Gustaf Mannerheim has been shoved unceremoniously into a distant forest clearing, rather than erected in the town centre. The city's left-leaning reputation is signified more subtly with the location of the **Central Museum of Labour** inside the former Finlayson dye works, which charts the changing lifestyle of a fictional Finnish working-class family, from the 1830s to the 1920s. Similar proletarian glories can be found in Amuri, the district that was the very edge of town in the 1890s, and hence whimsically named for the Amur River in Siberia on the border with China – then regarded as the edge of the world. Barely ten minutes' walk from the town centre, this former outlying region is now home to the **Amuri Museum of Workers' Housing**. The **Lenin Museum** is a small but perfectly formed commemoration of the Russian leader, built at the site where he first met Stalin. The Cold War gets a fun remembrance of its own at the **Spy Museum**, which deftly mixes a serious narrative of the history of espionage with hands-on examples to try. The **Metso Tampere City Library** includes a permanent exhibition of Moominabilia, sure to appeal to fans of Tove Jansson. Among many other museums, the town also boasts a museum complex, **Museum Centre Vapriikki**, where a single-admission ticket secures access to a number of world-class touring exhibitions (including, in the past, the Terracotta Warriors), and also a bunch of permanent on-site mini-museums that might not necessarily have enough pull on their own – but now you've bought your ticket, can you resist at least a quick glance at, say, the **Shoe Museum**?

The town's **Särkänniemi Theme Park** is full of rides and attractions, including the first **Angry Birds Land**, wringing yet more money from the pig-destroying video game.

Turku (Åbo)

'Barter' (*turgu*) in Old Slavic, and possibly simply 'The Residence' (*åbo*) in Old Swedish, the former capital of Finland has seethed in snooty resentment ever since the Russians relocated all the action to that glorified army camp, Helsinki. When its location on the south-western corner led unkind wags to call it 'the arse of Finland', the city tourist board fought back with an advertising campaign in which numerous celebrities exhorted viewers to 'Kiss my Turku'.

All of which makes the city sound like some over-defensive urban ruin, and not the rather charming Hanseatic town it is. It remains a delightful cultural centre of 'Swedish Finland', boasting the medieval **Turku Castle** at the mouth of the Aura River. Furnished today in rather a minimalist style, the castle is only truly rewarding to those who know what they are looking at – make the extra effort to take the guided tour, which really makes many otherwise bare rooms come to life with moments of Finnish history and culture.

Turku Cathedral also offers a glimpse of the medieval 'New Lands', much wrecked and rebuilt during numerous historical fires and remodellings, but still boasting the immense sarcophagus of Katarina Jagellonica, the Polish princess who brought a touch of class to the 16th-century regional centre. You will also find the grave of Samuel Cockburn, the Scottish mercenary who ended up as a local baron after loyal service to the Swedish crown. **Aboa Vetus** (Latin for 'Old Turku'), is built directly over the archaeological ruins of the medieval town, boasting not only authentic glimpses of the Turku of 800 years ago, but also a sad-looking mummified cat, thought to have been accidentally trapped in an in-filled cellar. For no discernable reason, this dead moggy has become something of a mascot for the museum. The modern art museum, **Ars Nova**, is on top of it, allowing the visitor to combine a single visit. **Turku Art Museum** contains some deeply impressive National Romantic images from the Golden Age of Finnish Art. Any tourist who is approaching Finland through the images of the *Kalevala* and its commentators will find as many, if not more, items here to interest them than they would in Helsinki.

The **Archipelago Sea** is the name often given to the thousands of island, skerries and shoals that scatter out towards the south-west – depending on how you want to count your islands, arguably the largest archipelago on the planet. Linked by a chain of free ferries in the summer, and by ice-roads in the winter, they make for a pleasant and picturesque excursion. The usual way to see them is to drive along the Archipelago Ring Road, around 200 kilometres of roads and ferry-crossings linking the largest and most inhabited islands.

Vaasa (Vasa)

A fire in 1852 wiped out the late medieval Swedish castle town, but mercifully left the palatial 18th-century French-classical Vaasa Court of Appeal intact. During the town's reconstruction, it was converted into **Mustasaari Church**, still home to the **Korsholm Music Festival**. The rebuilt town was known as Nikolaistad in honour of Tsar Nicholas I, for the rest of the period of Russian rule, snatching back its original name on the morning after the Russian Revolution in 1917. A **Statue of Freedom** in the town centre marks the town's pivotal role as the temporary headquarters of the

White government and military during Finland's revolution and civil war.

The **Ostrobothnian Museum** (*Pohjanmaan Museo*) charts the life of the municipality from medieval times onwards, favouring its importance as a Swedish regional centre – still relevant in a region where one in five locals still speaks Swedish as a first language. Vaasa's sufferings in various wars, from the War of Clubs peasant uprising of the 1590s, to the Revolution that saw the Grafton Rifles broken out of mothballs, are commemorated here.

Vantaa (Vanda)

The site of Helsinki airport is also home to the **Finnish Aviation Museum** and **Heureka**, the Finnish Science Museum. Like its London counterpart, Heureka is riddled with hands-on demonstrations and experiments, such as the chance to watch a team of mono-coloured rats take on a team of multi-coloured rats at basketball.

Appendix: The Lost Lands

Fully ten per cent of the lands once thought to be Finnish are now part of Russia. This includes the nickel-rich Arctic mining region of Petsamo, and the heartland of Karelia, seedbed of the *Kalevala* and ancestral home of many modern Finns.

The Karelian refugees are not visible to the average visitor, although their presence is palpable to anyone who gets to know a Finn well enough to ask where they are from. Everybody, it seems, has a grandparent or an uncle whose family were among the many thousands who fled the Soviets, thronging to Finland in the 1940s and swiftly integrating into local society. The immense logistic nightmare of receiving and resettling some 410,000 refugees (12% of the Finnish population) is a largely unmentioned story in

English-language narratives, although it occasionally finds official commemoration (see Gazetteer: Iisalmi).

Pechenga (Petsamo)

The 'lost arm' of the Maid of Finland, Petsamo was once the site of the northernmost monastery in the world, before it was evacuated in WW2 and its monks relocated to New Valamo (see Gazetteer: Iisalmi). The Russian interest in reclaiming the area was largely stirred by the discovery of rich nickel mining seams nearby, in what is now the township of Nikel. Occasionally wreathed in toxic fumes, Nikel is visible from Norwegian Lapland across the border, which is as close as any tourist is liable to want to venture.

Petrozavodsk (Äänislinna)

Although some Finnish tour companies offer long-haul coach trips over the border, a direct flight from Helsinki is the most convenient way to reach the Russian city of Petrozavodsk, capital of the Russian Republic of Karelia and once briefly the Finnish town of Äänislinna. Since the fall of the Soviet Union in the 1990s, the city has been swift to play up its tourist credentials as a summer lakeside resort and 'Christmas town' in winter. The **Kizhi Museum** features both restored old buildings and an Exhibition Centre containing actual exhibits.

Priozersk (Käkisalmi/Kexholm)

Torkel Knutsson, founder of Vyborg, also legendarily established an island-fort where one branch of the Vuoksi river from Lake Saimaa meets Lake Ladoga. Lost to Russia in the Great Northern War, but restored to Finnish authority when Finland became a Russian Grand Duchy, the town was first mentioned in Russian chronicles as Korela as early as 1140. It is notable today for the squat, round tower of **Korela Fortress**, said to have been founded by Torkel in the 1290s, but likely to have been a *Russian* stronghold before it was repurposed by the Swedes. The small castle museum recounts the fort's Swedish and Russian history. The Russians later converted it into a prison, where some of the 1825 Decembrist rebels were confined – little of its 'Finnish' history is apparent. The site is no longer an island, since the river level has fallen drastically in the last millennium. Modern materials, including red bricks, have been used in the 'restoration' of some of the medieval buildings.

Sortavala

This town on the banks of Lake Ladoga is the embarkation point for boats going to the **Orthodox Monastery** on the island of Valaam (see Gazetteer: Iisalmi). As one of the holiest sites in Orthodox Christianity, it remains a pilgrimage site for many Finns, and is hence liable to feature on many Karelian travel itineraries that originate in Finland. Mrs Tweedie dropped in to gently patronise the locals:

> Two hours' steam over the northern portion of that enormous lake brought forty islands, which form a group called *Valamo*, in sight, with the great white and blue-domed Russian church standing out clearly against a lovely sky. This building took four years to finish. The monks built nearly all of it themselves, made the bricks, carved the wood, painted the walls, ceilings, etc., and did all the goldsmith's work for lamps and altars. It is very massive, very great, catholic in its gaudy style, but sadly wanting tone. Much may, however, be accomplished by the kindly hand of time, which often renders the crudest things artistic, as it gently heals the wounds of grief.

Vyborg (Viipuri)

'Passing the old castle of *Wiborg* with its modern red roof and many centuries of Swedish history, then the palace of the Governor, to say nothing of numbers of villa residences further on, where the folk of St. Petersburg – only two hours distant by train – settle down for the summer to enjoy sea-bathing, we plunged into a charming pine-wood, through which the roadway was so narrow that the trees literally swished the carriage as it passed.' – Mrs Alec Tweedie, *Through Finland in Carts*.

Founded in 1293 by the Swedish crusader **Torkel Knutsson**, whose statue can be found near the castle bridge, the capital of Finnish Karelia fell into Russian hands as part of Old Finland province from 1721 to 1812, was reassigned to Finnish authority when all of Finland was incorporated as a Russian Grand Duchy, and formed the south-easternmost part of independent Finland after the collapse of imperial Russia. Too close to Leningrad for comfort, it and its surrounding region was snatched back by Russia in the Second World War.

If one wishes to be pedantic, one could point out that when Viipuri was 'founded', it was a castle imposed on a trading settlement that had previously owed allegiance to Novgorod – i.e. it was taken from the Russians in the first place. But no Finnish account is liable to consider this. At the time of its loss, Viipuri was Finland's second city, which has led to its enduring memory as the ancestral home of many thousands of modern Finnish families, descended from the refugees that fled it. As a result, it remains a popular tourist destination for Finns, and is a common stop, even if only for lunch, on coach trips from Finland to St Petersburg. The train from Helsinki also stops at Viipuri, affording travellers the chance to break their journey by going to see **Vyborg Castle**, now a museum.

The Alvar Aalto-designed **Vyborg Library** is also a popular destination for Finns, as is the **Statue of Lenin** in the town square, where passing Finns can be found scowling glumly at it. Vyborg once saw a considerably greater footfall of tourists from Finland – throughout the 1990s, cruise ships travelling the Saimaa Canal were permitted visa-free landings at the city. This was stopped in 2001, causing many (but not all) cruises from Savonlinna and Lappeenranta into the Gulf of Finland to speed past Vyborg without stopping. In what appears to be an attempt to lessen the annoyance, many choose to do so at night. If you go to the trouble of applying for a Russian visa, make sure your ship will actually stop there.

Zelenogorsk (Terijoki)

Now little more than a remote suburb of St Petersburg, this small town is on the line to Vyborg, although travellers will have to switch to a slow train to get there. This was once the Finnish Riviera town of Terijoki, transformed from a remote farming community at the turn of the 20th century into a heaving seaside resort playing host to summer hordes of 'dacha people'. More infamously, it also became the site of Otto Kuusinen's failed quisling government, the Finnish Democratic Republic, which even the Soviets ended up ignoring. It boasts two impressive Orthodox churches and a **Lutheran Church** built in 1909 when it was still Finnish. The yard of the latter still contains some 75 graves of Finns who died fighting against Russia in the Second World War. The customary **Statue of Lenin** waves a revolutionary hello, along with an odd **Monument to Dachshunds**. The **House of Novikov**, formerly the Karelian Isthmus border guards HQ and a Finnish officer's club, latterly the mansion where Kuusinen based his ill-fated government, is now a dilapidated ruin, in desolate disrepair.

Chronology of Major Events

1150   Supposed date of the legendary and probably fictional First Swedish Crusade in Finland.

1153   The English Cardinal Nicholas Breakspear is a missionary in Finland in the company of the Swedes.

1154   Nicholas Breakspear becomes Pope Adrian IV.

1155   Supposed date of the martyrdom of Saint Henry, murdered by Lalli the Finn.

1172   Pope Alexander III complains that Finnish Christians are lax in their devotions.

1220   The Englishman Thomas is appointed first bishop of Finland.

1237   Pope Gregory IX suggests a crusade 'in Tavastia' (Tampere/Hämeenlinna) to protect it from unidentified raiders – possibly Russians, but probably other Finns.

1240   'Swedish' attack on Novgorod is thwarted in the Battle of the Neva by Prince Alexander 'Nevsky', named for his victory.

c.1248 Second Swedish Crusade brings most of Finland
–50   under Swedish political control.

1293   Third Swedish Crusade leads to the conquest of Karelia and the establishment of Viipuri Castle.

1300   Consecration of the cathedral of Turku, Finland's original capital.

1319   Reign of King Magnus IV Ericson of Sweden.

1323   Treaty of Pähkinäsaari defines Finland's eastern
        border as a line drawn between the future site of St
        Petersburg and Oulu.

1346   A deal between bishops places the borders of the
        dioceses of Uppsala and Turku at Tornio, later used
        to mark the boundary between Finland and Sweden.

1353   The Black Death reaches Finland, killing an
        estimated third of its population.

1356   Reign of King Eric XII of Sweden.

1362   Reign of King Hacon of Sweden.

1364   Reign of King Albert of Sweden.

1389   Reign of Queen Margaret of Denmark, Norway and
        Sweden (including Finland).

1396   Reign of King Eric XIII.

1397   The Kalmar Union – Finland is the easternmost
        march of a united Fenno-Scandinavia, but is
        marginalised by the move of the overall capital to
        Denmark.

1441   Reign of King Christopher.

1448   Reign of King Charles VIII.

1457   Reign of King Christian I.

1497   Reign of King John II.

1520   Reign of King Christian II 'the Tyrant'.

1523   Reign of King Gustav I Vasa, end of Kalmar Union.

1524   Gustav Vasa splits from the Church of Rome;
        beginnings of Lutheranism as the state religion of
        Sweden and Finland.

1548   Mikael Agricola translates the New Testament into
        Finnish. Beginning of Finnish as a written language.

1550   Founding of Helsingfors (Helsinki), as a colony of
        new settlers from Hälsingaland in Sweden.

1557   The English sea captain Stephen Borrough draws up
        a list of 96 Saami words. Beginnings of Saami as a
        written language.

1560   Reign of King Eric XIV.

1562 Katarina Jagellonica, the Polish wife of the Duke of
      Finland, introduces Turku to foreign innovations
      including the fork and the napkin.
1569 Reign of King Johan III of Sweden, former Duke
      of Finland. The deposed mad King Eric XIV is
      imprisoned in several castles, including Turku.
1590 Tsar Boris Godunov invades Finland, initiating the
      Russo-Swedish War.
1592 Reign of King Sigismund of Sweden.
1596 Peasant uprising known as the War of Clubs,
      suppressed in 1597 by Clas Fleming.
1604 Reign of King Karl IX of Sweden.
1611 Reign of King Gustav II Adolf of Sweden.
1617 Treaty of Stolbova leaves Karelia in Swedish hands.
1632 Reign of Queen Christina of Sweden.
1642 First publication of the entire Bible in Finnish.
1654 Reign of King Karl X Gustav of Sweden.
1660 Reign of King Karl XI of Sweden.
1673 Joannis Schefferus writes his book *Lapponia*, at least
      partly to dispel rumours that the Swedish crown is
      employing Saami sorcerers in its foreign wars.
1673 Swedish proclamation states that Saami and farmers
      each have equal right to dwell in Lapland. Effective
      beginning of the colonisation of Saami lands in the
      north.
1695 Great Famine of Finland, also known as The Years
      of Many Deaths, in which 15–20% of the Finnish
      population perishes in just 24 months.
1697 Reign of King Karl XII of Sweden.
1700 Great Northern War between Sweden (and its allies)
      and Russia (and its allies).
1718 Reign of Queen Ulrika Eleonora of Sweden.
1720 Reign of King Frederick I of Sweden, with Ulrika as
      queen consort.
1721 Great Northern War ends with Sweden's loss of its
      territories on the south shore of the Gulf of Finland

(including modern-day Estonia), and parts of Karelia (known as 'Old Finland' in Russia).

1751 Reign of King Adolf Frederick of Sweden.

1771 Reign of King Gustav III of Sweden.

1792 Reign of King Gustav IV Adolf, last Swedish monarch to rule Finland.

1808 Outbreak of the Finnish War between Sweden and Russia.
Russian forces occupy Finland.

1809 Finland becomes a Grand Duchy of Russia, under Tsar Alexander I.

1812 Helsinki becomes the new capital of Finland.
The eastern lands of 'Old Finland' (lost in earlier wars) are restored to the Finnish Grand Duchy in order to streamline administration.

1819 The Scottish Quaker James Finlayson sees the Tampere rapids, and applies for permission to build a cotton mill powered by the waters.

1823 James Finlayson completes his first factory in Tampere.

1825 Nicholas I becomes Tsar.

1827 The Great Fire of Turku destroys Finland's largest town. Many institutions, including the university, are permanently relocated to Helsinki, hastening Turku's decline from its former prominence.

1835 First edition of Elias Lönnrot's *Kalevala*.

1836 James Finlayson sells his interest in the Tampere cotton mills, which retain his name.

1848 Publication of *Tales of Ensign Stål* by Johan Ludvig Runeberg.
First performance of the de facto Finnish national anthem 'Maamme' (Our Land), with lyrics by Runeberg and tune by Fredrik Pacius.

1849 Revised edition of the *Kalevala*.

1852 In Guovdageaidnu (Kautokeino), Norway, a group of Saami religious fanatics kill a merchant and policeman. Retroactively cited as the first event of Saami dissent.

1853   Outbreak of the Crimean War.

Laestadians are ordered to have their own separate church services: effective beginning of Laestadianism as a distinct splinter from Christianity.

1854   In order to blockade St Petersburg and divert Russian forces from Crimea, an Anglo-French squadron attacks targets in the Baltic Sea, including controversial bungled raids on the Finnish coast.

1855   Anglo-French siege and bombardment of the naval fortress at Suomenlinna.

Alexander II becomes 'the Good Tsar'.

End of Crimean War.

1856   The Saimaa Canal connects Finland's largest lake and its tributaries to the sea at Viipuri.

1860   Russian rouble replaced by the Finnish *markka* as local currency.

1865   A wood-pulp mill is founded by Frederik Idestam in Tampere.

1866   A wet summer and hard winter lead to a new famine, recorded in Finnish accounts as the Great Hunger Years. 15–20% of the Finnish population dies by 1868.

1868   To secure hydroelectric power, Idestam relocates his mill to the nearby town of Nokia. The company takes its name from its new location.

1875   Publication of the *Book of Our Country*, by Topelius.

1877   The Plevna weaving hall in Tampere is the largest in the Nordic countries, with 1,200 power looms. It is the first in Finland to be fitted with electric lighting.

1881   Assassination of Alexander II. Succeeded by Alexander III.

1894   Death of Alexander III. Nicholas II becomes Tsar.

1898   Eduard Polón founds the Finnish Rubber Works (Gummitehdas).

1899   February Manifesto of Nicholas II asserts his right to rule Finland without consulting native authorities. Beginning of the unpopular *Russification* policies.

1900   The Language Manifesto mandates Russian as the language for Finnish institutions.
Sibelius completes his *Finlandia* symphony.

1901   Conscription Law obliges Finns to serve in the Russian army.

1902   Nokia adds electrical generation to its portfolio.

1903   Governor-General of Finland granted dictatorial powers.

1904   Assassination of Governor-General Nikolai Bobrikov.

1905   *John Grafton* Incident and defeat for Russia in the Russo-Japanese War.
First Russian Revolution leads to promises of reform.

1912   Arid Wickström founds the Finnish Cable Company.

1916   Finnish Jaeger volunteers fight for Germany; they will eventually return home to fight on the White side in the civil war.

1917   Second Russian Revolution; outbreak of Finnish revolution/civil war.
Finland declares independence from Russia.

1918   Otto Kuusinen declares the Finnish Socialist Workers' Republic, flees to Russia after his defeat by the Whites.

1926   First Finnish radio broadcasts.

1934   First edition of *Sápmelaš*, the first Saami newspaper in Finland.

1939   Frans Eemil Sillanpää wins Nobel Prize for Literature.
Outbreak of Winter War against Soviets (ends 1940).

Otto Kuusinen proclaims the Finnish Democratic Republic in Terijoki.

1941 Outbreak of Continuation War against Soviets (ends 1944). Finns and Nazis recapture much of Karelia, only to lose it once more.
Veikko Koskienniemi writes lyrics to accompany the hymn section of Sibelius's *Finlandia*.

1944 Lapland War against the Nazis. Destruction of most buildings north of Rovaniemi (ends 1945).

1945 *The Moomins and the Great Flood*, first of the Moomin books, originally published in Swedish.

1946 First Finnish radio broadcasts in Saami.

1948 Friendship, Cooperation and Mutual Assistance Treaty with Soviet Union.

1952 Helsinki Olympics unfortunately leads to the invention of the *lonkero*.

1956– Urho Kekkonen is president for much of the Cold
1981 War.

1958 First Finnish television broadcasts.

1960 Saami Affairs Committee founded to implement Finnish Saami policy at a ministerial level.

1967 Nokia, the Finnish Rubber Works and the Finnish Cable Company merge to form the Nokia Corporation. Its newly-founded electronics division will run at a loss for the next 15 years.

1971 Nokia initiates its Finnish network for 'car-phone radios.'

1977 Saami television broadcasts in Finland now run out of dedicated facilities in Inari.

1982– Mauno Koivisto is Finland's president through the
1994 collapse of the Warsaw Pact.

1984 Nokia buys its main telecommunications competitor, Salora.
Nokia's Mobira Talkman 'portable' phone retails at roughly US$ 6,000.

1986 Design approved for a Saami flag.

1987   'Second generation' mobile technology, which
       allows international roaming and transmission of
       data (i.e. text messaging), brought in with Nokia's
       Global System for Mobile Technology (GSM) –
       internationally adopted.

1990   *Happy Moomin Family*, the third Japanese iteration
       of the *Moomin* cartoons, starts a 'Moomin Boom',
       leading to increased Finland tourism, particularly
       among the Japanese.

1991   Helsinki University student Linus Torvalds begins
       work on his own operating system, later known as
       Linux. Beginning of Finland's association with open-
       source software.

1992   Finns gain right to use the Saami language
       in dealings with the authorities in Lapland,
       although proficiency in the Saami language is only
       'recommended' for those same authorities.

1993   Finland founds a Saami Parliament for limited home
       rule.

1994– Martti Ahtisaari is president of Finland.
2000

1995   Finland joins the European Union.
       Law on Cultural Self-Government puts funding and
       control for local education in the hands of Saami.
       Social and health services added in 2002.

1998   Nokia is the world's largest mobile phone
       manufacturer, and remains so for the next 14 years.
       Santa Park opens near Rovaniemi.

1999   First Finnish euros minted.

2000– Tarja Halonen is president of Finland.
2012

2000   Helsinki is the European Capital of Culture.

2002   Official date of the replacement of the Finnish
       markka with the euro.

2005   Silvio Berlusconi proclaims that Finnish food is
       awful.

2006 Lordi wins the Eurovision Song Contest with 'Hard
      Rock Hallelujah'.

2007 Android and Apple iPhones bring lethal
      competition to Nokia in the mobile telecoms
      market.

2008 The Finnish-made 'Berlusconi' pizza beats Italy into
      second place in an international competition.

2009 Release of the first game in the *Angry Birds*
      franchise.

2011 Turku is the European Capital of Culture.

2013 Sauli Niinistö is president of Finland.
      Nokia's mobile phone business, the only major part
      left after the company divested itself of most other
      businesses in the 1990s, is sold to Microsoft.

2017 Centenary of the foundation of the Finnish republic.

Further Reading and References

U NLESS MY MAIN text is quoting from an untranslated source, all the books listed here are available in English. Many books concerning Finland are inadequately tagged by online booksellers, and only show up on searches if one directly requests them. Hence, the recommended reading lists common to Armchair Traveller's Histories are more useful than usual here, and may prove much more helpful to the tourist. Truly dedicated or interested readers are advised to browse the 'Fennica' sections in Finnish bookshops, which often have English-language translations of local books. Local museums and university bookstores are also liable to have locally-produced, small-press translations of books and theses that have never reached the attention of Amazon.

Guidebooks

There's nothing to fault the chunky *Lonely Planet: Finland* guide, most recently updated in 2012 and handily now available for the Kindle. However, the tourist who truly wants to investigate the forgotten corners of the country might like to invest in harder-to-find *Finland: A Cultural Guide* (Otava, 2003) by Pirkko-Liisa Louhenjoki-Schulman and Kaius Hedenström, which not only roots out the obscure art collections and craft centres, but also offers numerous illustrations to pique the interest and help the confused traveller.

Jorma Tuomi-Nikula and Altti Holmroos are the authors of *Finnish Inland Waters and Archipelago in the Wake of the Czars* (Kristina Cruises, 2003), which offers an English-language précis of Tuomi-Nikula's earlier Finnish-language book on the vacationing Tsars. It is an informative bilingual booklet about the routes taken by company cruise ships from Helsinki, way out west to the Åland Islands, and then all the way east on the Gulf of Finland to Viipuri, and up through the Saimaa canal as far as Savonlinna. Further details can be found at www.saimaacruises.fi

Publishers and Authors

Finns are avid readers, in several languages, although the small size of the population can make local books expensive. Many Finnish towns boast branches of **Suomalainen Kirjakauppa** (The Finnish Bookshop) and **Akateeminen Kirjakauppa** (The Academic Bookshop), both of which are sure to have an impressive selection of English-language novels and magazines. Many Finnish authors have been translated into English, as worthy literati, earnest representatives, or participants in the modern fad for Nordic Noir. There are in fact, so many available once you start looking, that a small book such as this can only barely scratch the surface.

Hard to find in English, but immensely influential on the Finns, is Johan Ludvig Runeberg's *Tales of Ensign Stål* (English trans. WSOY, 1952). Originally published in Swedish between 1848 and 1860, and recounting the events of the war that cost Sweden its *Eastland*, it has been translated four times into Finnish to reflect changes in language and attitude. It was a set text in schools in both Finland and Sweden. During the Winter War, it was reprinted and given away free to soldiers to instil a sense of nationalist spirit. Some of its opening verses, 'Maamme' (Our Land), were set to music and form the basis of Finland's modern national anthem.

Oh our land, Finland, land of our birth,
Rings out the golden word!
No valley, no hill,
No water, shore more dear
Than this northern homeland,
Precious land of our fathers.

Your splendour from its shell
One day will bloom;
From our love shall rise
Your hope, glorious joy,
And once your song, fatherland
Higher still will echo.

Runeberg is celebrated in many monuments throughout
Finland, and in the Runeberg Tart, one of the stodgy confec-
tions of which the Finns are inexplicably proud. He is oddly
unrepresented in the English language despite his importance; he not only gave Finland a martial epic of the end of
the Swedish era, but also *The Elk Hunters* – supposedly the
first valorisation of the common man in Finland, kicking off
a rich vein of national literature, and *King Fjalar*, an 'Ossi-
anic' poem, which is to say, a fake history that might well
have defined a whole generation of Finnish art if the *Kalevala* hadn't come along and trumped it.

'In the beginning, there was the marsh, the hoe, and Jussi.'
With such a simple, cinematic sentence, zooming in on the
lone crofter draining a swamp to break new farmland, Väinö
Linna commences his three-volume epic *Under the North
Star* (Aspasia, 2001–3). Encompassing several generations,
from the closing days of Russian rule to the aftermath of
the Second World War, it charts the fortunes of the Koskela
family as they create their homestead out of wilderness and
then stand their ground against predatory authorities, civil
strife and economic hardship.

Linna was one of the most influential Finnish authors

of the 20th century, in part for his controversial book *The Unknown Soldier* (WSOY, 1968). The abridged English edition lacks much of the feather-ruffling effect of the 1954 original, in which Linna drew on his own experiences in the Continuation War. Linna's soldiers are preoccupied with staying alive and hanging onto their dug-out – an action-oriented, subjective touch that was deeply out-of-step with other mythologies of the war, which would have their readers believe that everybody was a hero fighting out of deep-seated political convictions and a grasp of the bigger picture. In 2000, an earlier draft was published under his original title of *Sotaromaani* (*A War Novel*). Even more critical of the establishment and cynical about 'why we fight', it is sadly unavailable in English.

Tove Jansson remains a popular point of entry for foreign readers, although the author confesses that her world-famous *Moomin* stories leave him cold. The more one knows about Jansson's life, the more they look like extended Mary-Sue diaries, in which Jansson alleviates boredom in a summer shack by pretending all her lovers, family members and house-guests are eccentric trolls. Boel Westin's *Tove Jansson: Life, Art, Words – the Authorised Biography* (Sort Of Books, 2013) offers a more thorough portrayal of this most famous of Swedish-speaking Finns, whose books for adults are often overlooked. For a glimpse of her skills outside the children's market, see *Travelling Light*, *The Listener*, or her autobiography *Sculptor's Daughter: A Childhood Memoir*.

Written originally in Czech, Markéta Hejkalová's *Mika Waltari: the Finn* (WSOY, 2007) examines the career of the unassuming novelist who was once an international superstar. It is a firm reminder of how Anglophone success is not everything – Waltari has been translated into over 40 languages, although his historical epics such as *The Roman* and *The Etruscan* are little-known in English. *The Egyptian* was made into a film starring Yul Brynner, but Waltari sometimes seems excluded from the conversation on Finnish literature, because unlike many of his contemporaries, he rarely wrote on the Matter of Finland. He found pharaohs more interesting than farmers, and in the long run, that may have cost him his place in the Finnish hall of fame.

Several Finnish crime novelists have managed to clamber aboard the translation bandwagon for Nordic Noir, including Jarko Sipilä with his *Helsinki Homicide* series, and Harri Nykänen's *Raid* books – the latter featuring one of the most Finnish men imaginable, a good-hearted hitman who duels with evil Swedes in battles of wits, before sloping off to the forest to barbecue a celebratory sausage.

Antti Tuominen's *The Healer* (Vintage, 2013) straddles the line between thriller and science fiction, set in a near future Helsinki depopulated by climate change. As one might expect from the country whose very sense of self was bootstrapped out of a fantasy book, Finland's speculative fiction community is a busy bunch, most ably represented on the international stage by Johanna Sinisalo, author of *Troll* and *The Blood of Angels*. She is also the editor of the *Book of Finnish Fantasy* (Dedalus, 2005), which along with Desirina Boskovich's *It Came From the North* (Cheeky Frawg, 2013) offers a rogue's gallery of the genre's Finnish movers and shakers.

Finland also forms a backdrop for many novels by foreigners, such as Elizabeth Hand's *Available Dark* (Minotaur, 2012), in which a photographer goes on the trail of heavy metal murders. It is a location for both the film and original book of Len Deighton's *Billion-Dollar Brain* (Cape, 1966), and makes little impression in Raymond Benson's abysmal *Icebreaker* (Cape, 1983) in which James Bond visits Helsinki and singularly fails to evoke any sense of place or character.

General Accounts

The chunkiest and most in-depth general account in English is Eino Jutikkala and Kauko Pirinen's *A History of Finland*

(WSOY, 2003), now in its sixth edition. More concise, but wonderfully detailed and significantly cheaper, is Fred Singleton's *A Short History of Finland* (2nd ed., Cambridge University Press, 1998).

Places and Encounters

The seasoned Finland visitor will find much to enjoy in Tony Lurcock's surveys of a particular kind of foreign tourist. His *Not So Barren or Uncultivated: British Travellers in Finland 1760–1830* (CB Editions, 2010), and its sequel *No Particular Hurry: British Travellers in Finland 1830–1917* (CB Editions, 2013) collate a lifetime's collecting of obscure letters and journals, and mining them for their most pertinent or humorous soundbites – any travellers' quotes in this book not named in this bibliography are liable to have been lifted from Lurcock's anthologies.

For a more modern tour of the country, Robert Goldstein's *Riding With Reindeer: A Bicycle Ride Through Finland, Lapland and Arctic Norway* (Rivendell, 2011) sweetly recounts his numerous encounters with various winding roads, deceptively hilly dales, and politely disbelieving Finns as he cycles across the whole country in a haphazard zigzag.

Arts and Crafts

The most crucial art of Finnish culture in the 19th century is surely Elias Lönnrot's *Kalevala* (OUP, 1999), which only truly comes alive once one has seen the forests and lakes, and heard the rhythm of spoken Finnish at first hand. His later *Magic Songs of the Finns* (repr. Pagan Archive, 2011) is a fantastically detailed and cross-referenced collection of spells and stories, origin myths and curses, offering the curious reader everything from charms to protect against bears to bogglingly graphic spells to ease the pain of childbirth. He also lists kennings – poetic allusions – that recur in Finnish poetry, that speak volumes themselves with such revelations that a wolf was an 'Estonian cur', and a cockroach, somewhat less evocatively, was a 'six-footed, ball-shaped thing'.

Prehistory to 1159

There is remarkably little in English on Finnish prehistory; my main source is Matti Huurre's *9000 Vuotta Suomen esi-historiaa* (Otava, 2004). A general Arctic account, which includes Finland, can be found in John Hoffecker's *A Prehistory of the North: Human Settlement of the Higher Latitudes* (Rutgers, 2004). Otherwise, the best starting point is likely to be some of the anthropological materials listed below in the Saami section.

Swedish Finland: 1159–1809

The best account of the Christianisation of the Nordic countries is in Eric Christiansen's *The Northern Crusades* (Penguin, 1997), although it covers all the Baltic, not merely the region now known as Finland. But since the Finns for much of the period were intimately involved with the history of Sweden itself, as subjects of the Swedish crown, the best place to understand the Gustavs and the Adolfs of the era is somewhere like *A Concise History of Sweden* (Cambridge University Press, 2008), by Neil Kent. Karl XII, 'last of the Vikings', and his amazing life in the saddle are covered in great depth in Robert Nisbet Bain's *Charles XII and the Collapse of the Swedish Empire* (Putnam, 1895), now widely available in facsimile and e-Book reprints. For a more modern take on the era when Finnish cavalrymen fought at the edges of the Ottoman Empire, Gary Dean Peterson's *Warrior Kings of Sweden* (McFarland, 2007) has plenty of swashbuckling and scandal.

Aboa vetus et nova (Suomen Kirjallisuuden Seura, 2005) is a large format book in four parallel languages – the original

Latin of Daniel Juslenius, as well as Finnish, Swedish and English. A Master's thesis from 1700, seeking to reclaim as much lost history as possible after the destruction of the Duchy archives in a fire at Kuusisto in 1439, it remains one of the richest sources on medieval Finland, particularly Turku.

For a glimpse of some of the activities in the period's wars, Reijo Heikkinen's *Kajaani Castle* (Kainuu Museum, 2005) approaches through the rise and fall of the titular site. Matti Laamanen and Hanna-Leena Prusi achieve something similar with *Olavinlinna Castle* (National Board of Antiquities, 2007), which details everything to be found at Savonlinna's titular keep.

Reimund Kvideland and Henning Sehmsdorf's *Scandanavian Folk Belief and Legend* (Minnesota University Press, 1988) includes many folktales from Swedish-speaking Finland, relics of the period when the country was a Swedish province.

Russian Finland: 1809–1917

Nineteenth century Finland's greatest foreign chronicler is Mrs Alec Tweedie, the charmingly racist but often insightful woman of letters whose *Through Finland in Carts* (Thomas Nelson & Sons, 1897) remains oddly up-to-date in its assessment of the Finnish character. Although I have quoted her extensively regarding particular places in the Gazetteer, the bulk of her observations are about Finnish people and the natural world, and richly rewarding to the modern visitor, because so little appears to have changed.

The story of the Crimean War in the Baltic is told in exhaustive detail by Basil Greenhill and Ann Giffard in *The British Assault on Finland 1854–1855: A Forgotten Naval War* (Conway, 1988).

The story of Russian Finland is also, inevitably, the story of the development of Finnish nationalism, particularly through the compilation, publication and reception of Elias Lönnrot's

Kalevala. Juha Pentikäinen's *Kalevala Mythology* (Indiana University Press, 1999) is not only an in-depth guide to the epic itself, but also an incisive biography of its author and the very personal experiences and inspirations that inspired his text. *Sibelius: A Composer's Life and the Awakening of Finland* (University of Chicago Press, 2009) does much the same thing for the music of Finland's national composer.

For anyone looking for a truly deep study of the period, Derek Fewster's *Visions of Past Glory: Nationalism and the Construction of Early Finnish History* (Finnish Literature Society, 2005) picks apart the different strands and applications of Finnish national identity, not only during the Russian period but also in the 20th century as the Finns struggled to reconcile their changing political situation to similarly variable historical records and artistic works. Fewster identifies shades of meaning and interpretation that a book like this one can only hint at. Tuomo Polvinen's *Imperial Borderland: Bobrikov and the Attempted Russification of Finland* (Hurst, 1995) is similarly comprehensive on the complex politics of the late 19th century, as Russia's tightening fist caused so much goodwill to slip from its grasp.

Finland in the 20th Century

Anthony Upton's *The Finnish Revolution 1917–1918* (University of Minnesota Press, 1980) is a chunky 600-page account of the upheaval also known as the Finnish Civil War, rich with anecdotes and detail. Very little about the Reds exists, since those most likely to commemorate them were either dead in 1918, exiles in Russia, or emigrants to the USA and elsewhere. There is, however, Petri Haapala et al's *Tampere 1918: A Town in the Civil War* (Vapriikki, 2010), published by the town museum, crammed with evocative photographs and essays on the various elements of the war and its aftermath. Rüdiger von der Goltz, a leader of the German troops in Finland during the civil war, published his memoirs of the period as *My Mission in Finland and the Baltic* (Koehler, 1920); translator Peter Kalnin published the entire work as an e-book in 2013, available from Amazon.

The sorry tale of the scramble to cook up a Finnish king is best told in English in Michael Nash's article 'The Last King of Finland' (*Royalty Digest* 2012: 1). A far more in-depth account, only available in Finnish, is Martti Santavuori's *Suomen kuningas* (Karisto, 1965).

My own *Mannerheim: President, Soldier, Spy* (Haus, 2009) is a biography of Finland's most famous leader, including his early life in Russian military service, his leadership of the White forces in the civil war, and his triumphant days as the Marshal of Finland.

Finland's wartime history is told in many books, although perhaps the most comprehensive in English is William Trotter's *Winter War* (Aurum, 2003, released earlier in the US as *A Frozen Hell*). Once into the rarefied realms of military publishing, there is an embarrassment of riches about Finnish armaments and vehicles, and stirring tales of veterans and soldiers.

British readers might like to seek out Justin Brooke's obscure book on his wartime experiences, *The Volunteers: The Full Story of the British Volunteers in Finland 1939–41* (Self Publishing Association, 1990). Tellingly, it had a mass-market publication in its original Finnish edition, but limped out from a vanity press in the author's homeland. More farce than force, it tells the tale of several hundred British men, many deemed unfit for service at home, others instilled with a romantic notion of fighting Communists, who formed a volunteer detachment and shipped out to Finland, only to discover that the Winter War was already over. The men see no action, at least of a military nature, although there are anecdotes galore about their adventures, including a drunken and unforgettably misguided attempt to curry favour with a waitress in Jyväskylä by buying her a pair of French knickers.

The Saami and Lapland

Various orthographies write their name as the Saami or the Sámi, so get used to calling them that, rather than 'Lapps,' which they regard as racist and derogatory – Lapland implies a location on the periphery, and a Lapp is hence by definition an outsider.

In terms of chunky books on Everything You Need to Know About the Saami, *The Saami: A Cultural Encyclopaedia* (SKS, 2005), edited by Ulla-Maija Kulonen, Irja Seurujärvi-Kari and Risto Pulkkinen is hard to beat. Its 500 pages offer entries on everything from *afruvvá* (mermaids) to *yoik* (song) and all parts in between. For a more narrative account, Veli-Pekka Lehtola's *The Sámi People: Traditions in Transition* (Kustannus-Puntsi, 2004) offers a concise history of the people of Lapland, from their earliest mentions in classical geographies, to their modern struggles over identity and representation.

Finland Today

Although it begins with the newly independent state in 1918, the bulk of George Maude's *Aspects of the Governing of the Finns* (Peter Lang, 2010) is concerned with the often-overlooked period of the Cold War – it is particularly good on the brinkmanship of the Kekkonen era, which is a fundamental cornerstone of Finnish historical memory, but almost entirely unknown to outsiders.

English subtitles are not forthcoming for local films in Finnish cinemas, but almost all Finnish films have English subtitles on their DVD release, and can present an interesting and enduring window into the culture for the visitor in search of different souvenirs. Pietari Kääpä's *Directory of World Cinema: Finland* (Intellect, 2012), offers an exhaustive run-down of the history, industry and outlook of Finnish film, although some of his contributors seem oddly keen on wittering in academic cant, while neglecting to mention that the particular film they are discussing is tediously unwatchable.

Beyond the internationally famous works of Aki Kaurismäki, and every year's seasonal crop of earnest but dull movies about Finnish urban decay or wacky outsiders, here are a few Finnish obscurities that may strike your fancy in the bargain bin. This list is by no means exhaustive; it merely represents some of the author's own discoveries, sure to leave echoes of Finland – good, bad and ugly – resounding in your lounge long after your return home.

Etulinjan Edessä (Behind Enemy Lines)
A bunch of Swedish-speaking Finns fight against the Russians during the Continuation War, with occasional breaks to discuss the point of it all, learn English, and read out speeches by Winston Churchill. Cameo appearance by Gustaf Mannerheim.

Into Eternity
A thought-provoking documentary about the ongoing construction of the Onkalo nuclear waste disposal site, framed as a time-capsule document for the people of the distant future.

Iron Sky
Possibly the most Finnish artefact ever created, crowd-funded by sci-fi fans with nothing better to do and a melting-pot of foreign film subsidies, and featuring a bunch of Moon-based Nazis returning to Earth in the near future and inadvertently becoming speech-writers for President Sarah Palin (no, really) before sparking a global crisis. Warning: contains jokes written by Finns and delivered by Germans.

Jadesoturi (Jade Warrior)
An attempt to mix the *Kalevala* with kung-fu legend, resulting in a muddled and pointlessly obtuse martial arts epic by someone who thinks it's cool not to know what the hell is

going on. Two men hit each other with hammers, and then someone has their head tied to a wolf.

Joki (River)

Like Robert Altman directing *Donnie Darko*, the same 15-minute period in an average Finnish town is seen from a dozen different interlocking viewpoints, as a lonely mother decides to kill herself, a man finds his wife is having an affair, an old couple face death, a surgeon tries bungee jumping, a girl insists on watching her boyfriend on the toilet, and a pizza cook finds love in the kitchen.

Kuutamolla (Under the Moon)

A red-haired Finnish girl obsessed with *Star Wars* meets the man of her dreams in a bittersweet tale of love over the cheese counter. Meanwhile, her mother runs a touring exhibition of photographs of men's willies. Supposedly this is the second in the 'Restless' trilogy, which means you can expect everyone to have sex with everyone else by the end.

Menolippu Mombasaan (One-Way Ticket to Mombasa)

Two fun-loving lymphatic cancer patients bust out of their ward, planning to busk, con and blag their way to Lapland, although initially they don't get much further than Kuopio, where they are immediately mistaken for skinheads. More fun than it sounds; includes comedy Goths and jokes at the expense of Lapland and Japanese tourists. Doesn't really have much to do with Mombasa.

Nousukausi (Upswing)

A bored Finnish yuppie couple take the 'holiday of a life-time' by volunteering to live on welfare for a fortnight in a Helsinki council estate. Additional unintentional comedy is added by the Finnish concept of a 'poverty line', which appears to be getting 300 euros a week in handouts. This was unique among Finnish movies I have seen in that it did not attempt any subtle references to cheese. The leading woman, however, does embark on an extended elegy to faucets – Finns are oddly obsessed with mixer taps.

Raid
Fantastically entertaining TV show and movie about a Swedish-Finnish hardman and the big fat cop who wants to bring him to heel, but also respects him for his maverick approach to justice. Includes a weirdo who thinks he's permanently at a football match, a topless Finnish girl extolling the virtues of porridge and a denouement (for the movie) in which Raid gets the girl, but then decides he would be better off heading out into the woods on his own and having a barbecue.

Rare Exports
Quirky combination of Christmas and horror, as reindeer herders in the frozen north uncover an underground vault where the *real* Santa Claus is kept locked up in chains.

Rauta Aika (Age of Iron)
Slow but ultimately fascinating TV-series retelling of the *Kalevala*, with some interesting decisions in terms of rituals, interpretations and the depiction of the Sampo.

Rukajärventie
Supposedly the best Finnish film ever made (according to the box), although the voting seems to have been largely conducted by Finnish maiden aunts who appreciate the highly gratuitous oral sex scene. Boy meets girl, boy loses girl, boy leads party of Finnish soldiers behind enemy lines to blow up Russians.

Sensuela
A Nazi pilot crash-lands in Lapland during the Continuation War, where he has a brief fling with a beautiful Saami

reindeer-sled racer. They rekindle their romance after the war in swinging Helsinki, where the innocent girl is soon plunged into psychedelic sexploitation miasma of lava lamps, garish curtains and wild parties. Possibly the worst film ever made, and hence possibly also the best.

Talvisota (Winter War)

Although it feels longer, this is only three hours. A group of brave Finns defend the land from evil Russians, and must cope with sub-zero temperatures, enemy bombardment and the absence of mixer taps. Relief eventually comes when someone builds a sauna, and two local alcoholics discover it's possible to drink the Molotov cocktails.

Vieraalla Maalla (Another Country)

An undercover sociologist posing as a foreign exchange student falls in love with the woman who is teaching him Finnish. High-jinks ensue when he is kidnapped by evil hicks and forced to fake his own death after escaping through a toilet in a Finnish holiday shack. Includes some comedy business with a goat.

Viimenen Neitsi Espoossa (Last Virgin in Espoo)

A pair of dim Finnish girls go on the run, intending to lose their virginity somewhere in Finland. It takes longer than you might expect.

Index